KU-746-029

MADRID

1989/1990 Edition

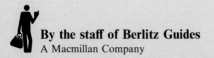

By the staff of Berlitz Guides

A Macmillan Company

How to use this guide

- All the practical information, hints and tips that you will need before and during the trip start on page 99.
- For general background, see the sections Madrid and the Madrileños, p. 6, and A Brief History, p. 11.
- All the sights to see are listed between pages 17 and 49, with suggestions on day trips from Madrid from page 49 to 78.

  Our own choice of sights most highly recommended is pinpointed by the Berlitz traveller symbol.
- Entertainment, nightlife and all other leisure activities are described between pages 79 to 91, while information on restaurants and cuisine is to be found on pages 92 to 98.
- Finally, there is an index at the back of the book, pp. 126–128.

Although we make every effort to ensure the accuracy of all the information in this book, changes occur incessantly. We cannot therefore take responsibility for facts, prices, addresses and circumstances in general that are constantly subject to alteration. Our guides are updated on a regular basis as we reprint, and we are always grateful to readers who let us know of any errors, changes or serious omissions they come across.

Text: Ken Bernstein
Photography: Dany Gignoux
Layout: Doris Haldemann
We are particularly grateful to Mr. Juan Manuel Alvarez Gallo for his help in the preparation of this book. We also wish to thank the Spanish National Tourist Office for its valuable assistance.

4 Cartography: Falk-Verlag, Hamburg.

Contents

Photo, pp. 2–3: El Escorial

Madrid and the Madrileños

At an altitude of more than 2,100 feet, this boom town on the Castilian plateau is Europe's highest capital. The combination of high altitude and mountain breezes generates a unique atmosphere. The city is alive with light, the sunshine filtering down through a pale sky barely dense enough to float a cloud on.

Life starts right down on earth. Madrid is a hospitable hotbed of cafés and restaurants, theatres and nightclubs. This is the world capital of bullfighting. The shops are among the finest in Europe. But save strength for the cultural pursuits, starting with the Prado Museum and the Royal Palace. Then set forth on easy excursions to the other highlights of central Spain, towns, steeped in history, of infinite beauty and charm.

Like Brasilia, Washington or other "artificial" towns, the city of Madrid is a man-made capital conceived in political compromise. King Philip II promoted Madrid from a provincial town to his national command post in the middle of the 16th century at a time when his empire was still expanding. Since then, Madrid hasn't stopped growing. Latest reports show the population as being just under 4 million; the area, 205 square miles.

Madrid's business has always been government, but new industries have been drawn to the magnet of power. Today's *Madrileño* (inhabitant of Madrid) may work in

Beauties of Madrid: face in the flea-market crowd, fountain at sunset.

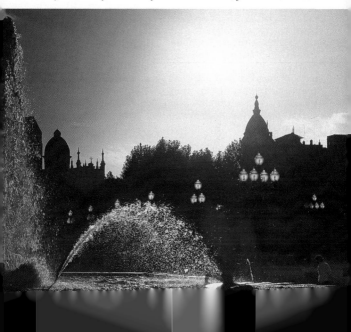

an engine or plastics factory, an insurance company's headquarters or a tourist hotel. With so much economic opportunity right in the geographical centre of the country, it's no wonder the capital is a melting pot of Spaniards from all over the nation. The young man you ask for directions may be a stranger here himself.

Don't be afraid of getting lost in Madrid. Outside every metro (underground) station there stands an oversize city map. Signs at bus stops explain where you're going and where the buses are coming from. The streets are well marked, often wittily, too, with illustrated wall tiles. A sign permanently displayed in a Puerta del Sol umbrella shop announces: *"Mañana lloverá"* (tomorrow it will rain). And if it doesn't, don't be disappointed. The streets are washed regularly with giant hoses.

Before the shrill traffic jams begin, early-morning Madrid sounds old-fashioned and neighbourly. A gypsy junkcollector chants his call. Caged canaries twitter. A grinding, tortured roar from a café means the espresso machine is boiling milk for **8** coffee. Europe's most sleepless

people, the *Madrileños,* are filing off to work only six hours after another late night out. The "night-people" image, no matter how deep-rooted, is not actually the real reason *Madrileños* are called *gatos* (cats). Academics claim the nickname originated in the 11th century when soldiers from Madrid spectacularly scaled the walls of an enemy fort, climbing like flies—or cats.

The city and its people run to extremes. It could well have something to do with the weather, which is usually either too cold or too hot (roughly one third of the population flees the city every August). The exaggerated contrasts extend to geography as well: the big city ends suddenly in open country, with no semi-detached suburbs to soften the edges. *Madrileños* seem to be bubbling one moment and sulking the next. They go to church but they go to the striptease, too. At a moment's notice, hand-kissing politeness gives way to the law of the jungle, for instance in the metro, where the train doors slam shut ten seconds after they open, and then, the devil take the hindmost. They may fume about the cost of living, but *Madrileños* never falter in their support of a thriving community of street beggars. They may bemoan the pace of modern life, but they find time to sit over coffee for an hour in an *tertulia,* or informal conversational club, discussing literature or football or the pace of modern life.

Observe the *Madrileños* cramming the promenades and outdoor cafés at the hour of the *paseo,* when the offices

A troubador troupe, called a tuna, *sets off to play in medieval garb.*

Winter scene, back-street Madrid: time changes only the wall slogans.

used to be given for fecundity) but they still take them everywhere. (Don't be concerned about the toddlers on the streets and in restaurants late at night, Madrid's junior ''cats'' make up for it at their afternoon siesta break.)

Enjoy Madrid in all its many aspects: human, historical, architectural and religious. There are enough museums alone to keep you busy for all your stay; but don't neglect the prodigious sights close enough for day trips. Be certain to see Toledo, Spain's former capital set on a crag, with its haunting memories of El Greco and with all Spain built into its houses and churches. Don't miss Segovia, a royal stronghold with its fairy-tale castle and classic Roman aqueduct. Tour the ancient walled city of saints, Avila. Closer to Madrid, you have to visit the Escorial, monastery, college and palace built for Philip II, and on the way, stop at El Valle de los Caídos (the Valley of the Fallen), Spain's memorial to her soldiers killed in the Civil War of 1936–39.

Situated as it is, in the epi-centre of Spain, Madrid is the perfect base for explorations into the heart and soul of the country.

begin to empty. Elegant businessmen escort impeccably coiffed women of all ages. And all those children in tow! Spaniards may be having fewer children (official awards

A Brief History

Until its sudden elevation to the status of capital city in 1561, the history of Madrid was long but undistinguished.

Remains from the Paleolithic, Neolithic and Bronze Ages have been unearthed in the Manzanares Valley around Madrid. The prehistoric population evidently appreciated the district's fresh air and water resources.

Nevertheless, even in the local scheme of things, Madrid's significance was negligible over many centuries crucial to the development of the Spanish people. The Romans built their most advanced province on the Iberian peninsula, but left no monuments in Madrid. Armies of North African nomads, spreading the Muslim religion in a relentless tide, invaded the peninsula in A.D. 711. Within ten years, they had overrun almost all of Spain. If Madrid played any role in this, no record of it remains.

The first solid references to this obscure settlement on the Castilian plateau, guarded by the brooding Guadarrama mountain range, don't appear until the 10th century. Even the name is vaguely recorded—perhaps Magerit or Magrit, but close enough to Madrid. The hamlet is mentioned in the chronicles because of its military significance, near the main line of resistance to the Christian reconquest. Since the struggle was to last for centuries, the defending Muslim army had time to build a full-scale fort, or *alcázar,* on the heights of Madrid commanding the Manzanares Valley.

Time passed and the crusading spirit driving south could not be held back forever. After several unsuccessful skirmishes, the Christian forces of Alfonso VI captured Madrid in 1083. The Alcázar became a fort of the Crown of Castile. During a counter-offensive a few years later, the town was overrun by the Muslims, but the Christianized Alcázar held, and shortly afterwards, the Moors were expelled once more, this time for good. But they were not to be driven from southern Spain for nearly another four centuries.

Meanwhile, Madrid enjoyed prominence for a short while in 1308 when King Ferdinand IV and his Cortes, an early version of parliament, held a formal meeting in the town. From then on, the kings of Spain began to visit

Madrid, where the air was invigorating and the hunting excellent.

Ferdinand and Isabella, known in Spain as the Catholic Monarchs who united all the provinces of Spain, first appeared in Madrid in 1477. They appreciated the town's loyalty to the Crown, but the idea never occurred to anyone, let alone the two monarchs, that Madrid might one day become the capital. Toledo served quite well enough.

Spain's Golden Age

Under Ferdinand and Isabella, Spain changed dramatically. In one year alone (1492), the royal pair presided over the discovery of the New World, the final conquest over the Moors, and the expulsion of the Jews. The country was entering its Golden Age, nearly a century of Spanish economic and political supremacy, accompanied by marvels of art and literature.

Ferdinand and Isabella per-

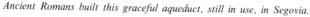
Ancient Romans built this graceful aqueduct, still in use, in Segovia.

sonify Spanishness (*Hispanidad*). By contrast, their grandson, who assumed the throne in 1516, was as un-Spanish as it is possible to imagine. Born in Flanders in 1500, Charles I could barely express himself in Spanish. The first of the Hapsburgs, he packed his retinue with Burgundian and Flemish nobles. Soon after his arrival in Spain, the young man inherited the title of Holy Roman Emperor, as Charles V; this crown necessarily kept him busy away from the royal residences of Toledo, Segovia, Valladolid and Madrid. While the monarch was away on one of his many business trips, his increasingly dissatisfied subjects protested violently. The revolt of the *comuneros,* or townsmen, broke out in a number of Spanish cities, including Madrid. The rebels occupied the Alcázar, which had by then been converted to a royal palace. The insurrection was put down and the leaders executed, but the king got the message. He tried thereafter to pay more attention to his Spanish constituency.

Madrid's Rise to Capital
In 1556, Charles abdicated in favour of his son, Philip II, which was good news for Spain and even better for Madrid. Philip proclaimed Madrid his capital in 1561, converting an unimpressive town of less than 15,000 into the headquarters of the world's greatest empire of the time. For Madrid, the future soared onwards and upwards; for Spain, upwards, then downwards. Philip II takes credit for the rousing naval victory at Lepanto (Spaniards and Venetians versus the Turks), but only 17 years later he allowed Spain to be subjected to the humiliating defeat of its "invincible" Armada at the hands of Sir Francis Drake and the small English navy. He left behind him as a monument the Escorial, the visionary super-palace and monastery in the foothills of the Sierra de Guadarrama, north-west of Madrid.

Philip's son, Philip III, was unfaithful to Spain's new capital. For several years he held court in Valladolid, though eventually he returned to Madrid. It was he who organized the construction of the Plaza Mayor—the magnificent main square which still dignifies the centre of the city. Other tasteful, 17th-century buildings nearby, such as the Foreign Ministry and the Town Hall, show that the cap- **13**

Reflection in a pool: Don Quixote statue in Madrid hails Cervantes.

ital was at last being taken seriously.

The Hapsburgs bowed out in 1700 with the death of Charles II. The subsequent War of the Spanish Succession resulted in the enthronement of the Bourbon candidate, Philip V. When the Alcázar of Madrid burned down in 1734 (with the loss, incidentally, of many art treasures), Philip decided to make the best of a bad thing. He ordered a new palace, ever more lavish.

The result is Madrid's Royal Palace. You can tour it whenever Philip's descendant, King Juan Carlos I, is not using it for official ceremonies.

Madrid owes a lot to the civic-mindedness of Charles III, who ruled from 1759 to 1788. He paved and lit the streets, installed public fountains, built what became the Prado Museum, and laid out promenades and gardens.

Goya painted the next king, Charles IV, looking strangely like his transatlantic contemporary, George Washington. But Charles was much less successful in politics. His 20-year reign, weak at best, ended

Man of Action, Man of Letters

MIGUEL DE CERVANTES SAAVEDRA fought at the Battle of Lepanto (1571), was wounded, captured, imprisoned; he escaped, was enslaved and finally ransomed. Returning to Spain, he worked as an army quartermaster but spent several spells in jail on financial charges. Then, at the age of 58, he wrote the world's best-selling novel, *Don Quixote*.

In his modest house in Madrid's Calle del León, Cervantes died on April 23, 1616, perhaps the saddest day in literary history—for on the same date, the world also lost William Shakespeare.

in all-round disaster: abdication, arrest and war.

Napoleon invaded Spain and invested his older, taller and more agreeable brother, Joseph, as King José I. On May 2, 1808, Madrid rose up against the interloper. The Peninsular War (called by the Spaniards the War of Independence) went on murderously, but inconclusively for six years. Finally, with the help of the British under the Duke of Wellington, the Spanish expelled the occupying forces. In truth, Joseph Bonaparte meant well—he built so many plazas that the *Madrileños* nicknamed him *El Rey Plazuelas*—but the people loathed a government imposed from abroad. José I spent 17 years of exile in, of all unlikely places, New Jersey.

A modern-day horseman, in parade in Madrid, typifies Spanish pomp.

Monument to the national tragedy: Civil War memorial of Valle de los Caídos lies north-west of Madrid.

Decline and Decadence

The son of Charles IV, Ferdinand VII, was seated on his rightful throne in the Royal Palace of Madrid in 1814. But the war and the repercussions of the French Revolution had helped to create in Spain the nucleus of a liberal and national party. The power struggles at home and rebellious colonies abroad were symptomatic of the 19th century as a whole. By the time of the Spanish-American War of 1898, the empire of the Golden Age had been whittled to insignificance. King Alfonso XIII, who linked the 19th and 20th centuries, inaugurated the Madrid metro (its underground railway) and University City. But he was undone by the chronic unrest of his subjects. Neither constitutional government nor dictatorship proved workable and, in 1931, the king went into exile following anti-royalist results in municipal elections.

The Civil War

Under the new Republic, bitter, hard ideological conflicts divided parties and factions, with the church also involved. Finally, in 1936, a large section of the army under General Francisco Franco rose in revolt against the government. On Franco's side were monarchists, conservatives, the Church and the right-wing Falangists. Against him was a collection of republicans, liberals socialists, communists and anarchists.

The Civil War developed into one of the great causes of the 20th century with support for both sides coming from outside Spain. Often unaware of—or indifferent to—the particular Spanish origins of the struggle, many Europeans saw the Civil War as a crucial conflict between democracy and dictatorship, or from the other side, as a conflict between law and order and the forces of social revolution and chaos. The bloodshed lasted three years and cost several hundred thousand lives. Madrid was in Republican hands for most of the war, but the government was evacuated in the early stages of a Nationalist siege which, to the accompaniment of frequent bombing, lasted until March, 1939.

Even when the war ended, the hardship continued. But Spain's new *caudillo* (leader), Generalísimo Franco, managed to keep Spain out of the Second World War despite Hitler's efforts at persuasion. Spain was admitted to the United Nations in 1955, opening the gates to an overwhelming tourist invasion, with profound effects on both the economy and national mentality.

When Franco died in 1975, Prince Juan Carlos, the grandson of King Alfonso XIII, became monarch. The new king's commitment to democracy has brought Spain into line with the rest of Western Europe and assured the country of membership in the European Economic Community.

What to See

Madrid has so many facets that, for centuries, Spaniards have informally referred to it in the plural—*Los Madriles*.

Since there's so much to take in, you'll have to divide the *Madriles,* geographically or chronologically, horizontally or vertically. A good way to start is to sign on to one of the half-day guided tours to help get your bearings. Once you have a general idea of the layout of the town, you can set forth on your own according to your interests: art, history, shopping, nightlife, or all of them. Our suggestions follow.

But whatever else you do, begin by savouring the oldest of the *Madriles*. Start on foot in the heart of the original Madrid.

Old Madrid

Little is left of medieval Madrid except the mood. You feel it in the narrow streets which meander south from the Calle Mayor (Main Street). Dimly lit shops sell what they've always sold: religious habits, books, cheeses, military medals, statues, capes (Dracula-style or even for princesses). Artisans chip away at their woodwork. A gypsy beggar-woman, holding somebody else's baby, insistently asks for a coin. A waiter pins up the hand-written menu in the doorway of an inn. A greengrocer builds a pyramid of tomatoes. A blind lottery-ticket salesman, tapping his white cane to attract attention, recites a poem promising instant riches.

In its formalized version, Madrid's most famous lottery-ticket establishment faces the **Puerta del Sol** (Gate of the Sun). On big days, crowds of customers wait outside the shop called *La Hermana de Doña Manolita* (Mrs. Manolita's Sister). Some historic jackpot tickets have been issued here, and the clients are waiting for new miracles.

The gate from which the Puerta del Sol takes its name may have been decorated with

Spanish Dramatists

Spain's three top dramatists of the Golden Age make Shakespeare seem like something of a dawdler in contrast.

LOPE DE VEGA (1562–1635) devised a new three-act format and turned out in the region of 1,500 plays.

TIRSO DE MOLINA (1571?–1648) wrote over 300 plays, including the first about the world's most famous lover, Don Juan.

PEDRO CALDERÓN DE LA BARCA (1600–81) is credited with more than 100 comedies, tragedies and religious allegories.

Madrileños all three of them, these men had chequered careers. Lope de Vega joined the Armada. Tirso de Molina served as a monk on the island of Santo Domingo. Calderón enlisted as a cavalry man and was later ordained a priest.

Madrid's main square preserves the elegant 17th-century architecture.

a sculpted or painted sun design. But this is an academic point, for the gate—part of the ancient town wall—was torn down in 1570. For centuries, this plaza, hub of ten converging streets, has been Madrid's nerve-centre. All the radial highways of Spain are measured from Puerta del Sol, "Kilometre 0".

The no-nonsense, neo-Classical building on the south side of the square is headquarters of the security police.

Nonetheless, thousands of *Madrileños* gather here for a ritual every New Year's Eve. They try to swallow a dozen grapes while the clock atop the building strikes 12. Then pandemonium breaks out.

In the central area of Puerta del Sol, overpowered by all the traffic, is a statue based on Madrid's coat of arms. It shows a bear standing against a *madroño* tree (an arbutus, or strawberry tree). This same

gourmet bear is seen all over Madrid, on the rear doors of every taxi, for instance.

The **Plaza Mayor** (Main Square), a few blocks away, is an architectural symphony in bold but balanced tones. Broad arcades surround a cobbled rectangle 200 yards long and 100 yards wide. It was built in the beginning of the 17th century, based on the graceful style of Juan de Herrera—symmetry, slate roofs, slender towers. (Juan de Herrera was Philip II's architect, responsible for the Escorial.) Plaza Mayor may be entered by any of nine archways, but mercifully not by motor vehi-

City on the move: Madrid is an expanding urban centre in a time-less setting, with the Castilian plateau stretching into the distance.

Sunday in Madrid

Some cities have sedate Sundays. Not Madrid. Try to take in the excitement.

The Rastro. Sunday mornings, the streets of Old Madrid, beginning just south of the cathedral, are transformed into one of the world's biggest flea markets. Tens of thousands of bargain-minded *Madrileños* join the out-of-towners in pricing clothing, antiques, pots and pans, and junk of all sorts. Care to buy a used gas mask?

The Stamp Market. Hundreds of collectors assemble in the Plaza Mayor on Sunday mornings to buy and sell stamps, coins, banknotes, cigar bands and even used lottery tickets. Watch the enthusiasts with their tweezers and magnifying glasses.

The Book Fair. Just south of the Botanical Garden, the bibliophiles throng to open-air stalls along Calle de Claudio Moyano. New and used books bought and sold: trash, comics, foreign fiction and valuable old tomes.

So much for the morning. After drinks, snacks and, of course, lunch, you'll have to decide whether to watch Real Madrid play football, or go to a bullfight, or follow the race-horses at the Zarzuela Hippodrome.

cles. Until relatively recent years, this was the scene of pageants, bullfights, even executions—residents disposing of more than 400 balconies overlooking the square used to sell tickets for such events. A statue of King Philip III, who ordered the Plaza to be built, occupies the place of honour but is no obstacle to events—ranging from pop concerts to theatre festivals—which are organized from time to time by the municipality. Take a seat at one of the outdoor cafés in the square and enjoy the proportions of Madrid's most elegant architectural ensemble.

Further along Calle Mayor, the old Plaza de la Villa (City Hall Square) juxtaposes stately 16th- and 17th-century buildings of varied style. The Casa y Torre de los Lujanes (the House and Tower of the Lujanes), 16th-century Gothic, has an imposing stone portal. The **Casa de Cisneros,** built in the mid-16th century by a nephew of the intrepid inquisitor and warrior, Cardinal Cisneros, belongs to the ornate and delicate style of architecture known as Plateresque. Finally, the **Ayuntamiento** (City Hall) represents the Hapsburg era, with the towers and slate spires characteristic of the 17th-century official buildings all around Madrid.

There are more than 200 churches in Madrid, but very

Sightless lottery-ticket salesman hopes for big Christmas business. Below: lull in activity at Rastro.

few could be classified among the essential tourist attractions. Madrid is too young a city to have a great medieval cathedral. The present (provisional) cathedral of Madrid in Calle de Toledo, the **Catedral de San Isidro,** needed major rebuilding after severe damage in the Civil War. It has a massive dome, a single nave and, among many relics, the revered remains of the city's patron saint, San Isidro Labrador (St. Isidore the Husbandman).

Just down Calle de Toledo from the cathedral is the site of the **Rastro,** Madrid's phenomenal flea market, which buzzes with bargain-hunters every Sunday morning (see page 22). Also in the neighbourhood are some popular local tapas bars and the workshops of Madrid's artisans, from guitar makers to bookbinders.

A formidable Madrid church of the mid-18th century is the **Basílica de San Francisco el Grande** (Basilica of St. Francis of Assisi). The curved façade, an original version of a neo-Classic design, somewhat curtails the effect of the church's most superlative feature. Once inside, you'll realize that the dome is out of the ordinary. Indeed, its inner diameter of more than 100 feet exceeds the size of the cupolas of St. Paul's (London) and Les Invalides (Paris). Oversized statues of the apostles in white Carrara marble are stationed around the rotunda. Seven richly ornamented chapels fan out from the centre. In the Chapel of San Bernardino de Siena, notice the large painting above the altar, a lively scene of the saint preaching. The second figure from the right, dressed in yellow, is said to be a self-portrait of the artist, the immortal Francisco de Goya.

Another landmark of old Madrid is the Hospital de San Carlos (Calle de Santa Isabel 52). It has been renovated to house the **Centro de Arte Reina Sofía,** a venue for exhibitions of contemporary art.

Central Madrid

Except for the intensity of the traffic, the ample **Plaza de la Cibeles** is splendid. The fountain in the centre shows Cybele, a controversial Greek fertility goddess, serenely settled in a chariot pulled by two lions. The sculptural ensemble is probably the best-known fountain in all Spain.

Trees and fountains gracing Plaza de España ease Madrid pressures.

The most unavoidable building on the plaza is the cathedral-like Palacio de Comunicaciones, sarcastically nicknamed *Nuestra Señora de las Comunicaciones* (Our Lady of Communications). This ponderous post office, inaugurated in 1919, is dismal inside; its high ceilings, overhead walkways and general inhumanity give it the air of a prison.

While the Communications Palace shows off, the Army headquarters across the square camouflages itself behind 100-year-old iron railings. The army, improbably, occupies a huge mansion in

an enviable garden dotted with statues of scantily clad nymphs. This may explain why there are so many sentries guarding this coy private park.

Also facing Plaza de la Cibeles, the headquarters of the Bank of Spain combines neo-Classic, Baroque and Rococo styles. It looks about as solid as any bank can be. The financial district, Madrid's City, or Wall Street, begins here on **Calle de Alcalá.** Pompous buildings in this very high-rent district contain the head offices or branches of more than 100 banks plus insurance companies, the Finance Ministry and, a few streets away, the **Bolsa de Comercio** (Stock Exchange). Incidentally, the women selling lottery tickets are posted round the severely columned portal of the Stock Exchange, and suggest one more little gamble to arriving and departing tycoons.

But Calle de Alcalá is not entirely dedicated to Mammon. Next door to the Ministry of Finance is the clumsily named **Museo de la Real Academia de Bellas Artes de San Fernando**—call it the

Fountain and sculpture of Cybele glittering in the Madrid eventide.

Museum of the Royal Academy. The academy owns a celebrated batch of Goya's paintings, including the *Burial of the Sardine,* full of action and humour, and a superb self-portrait of the artist in his vigorous old age. Velázquez, Magnasco, Murillo and Rubens are also represented among hundreds of works on display.

And then there's the Royal Academy's magnificent collection of paintings by Zurbarán, which rivals that of the Prado. Representative of the artist's austere, devotional style are the *Vision of the Blessed Alonso Rodríguez* and a series of portraits of friars.

Now let's return to the **Gran Vía,** main east-west thoroughfare and lifeline of modern Madrid. The bustling Gran Vía (Main Avenue) is a mixture of hotels, shops, theatres, nightclubs and cafés—the street for strolling and window-gazing. Connoisseurs of traffic jams will appreciate the nightmarish rush-hour along this busy street. Pony-tailed policewomen frantically gesticulate and whistle in a doomed effort to stir the immovable traffic; drivers at their wit's end lean on their horns in sympathy and add to the cacophony. And a special bonus: in Madrid, thanks to the siesta break, the rush-hour happens not twice, but *four* times a day.

You can get your bearings on the Gran Vía by looking *up*. The highest tower in sight belongs to Madrid's first *rascacielos* (skyscraper), the headquarters of the telephone company. La Telefónica, as it is called, sprouts antennas and parabolic reflectors.

At **Plaza del Callao** (named after Peru's principal port), the pedestrian traffic reaches its peak. This is the centre for department stores, cinemas, cafés and bus stops: yet only a couple of streets south of Callao's turbulence, the **Convent of Descalzas Reales** clings onto a 16th-century tranquillity. The institution was founded by Princess Joanna of Austria, the daughter of Holy Roman Emperor Charles V, and subsidized by generous patrons. In 1961, it was opened to the public as a national museum. Cloistered nuns of the Santa Clara order, still on the premises, stay out of sight during visiting hours. As for tourists, their first view of the convent's splendours begins with the theatrical grand stairway. Upstairs are heavy timbered ceilings and walls covered with works of art, **29** mostly of religious or royal significance. In one hall, there are a dozen 17th-century tapestries based on original Rubens drawings. The museum contains outstanding paintings by Titian, Brueghel the Elder, Zurbarán and Sánchez Coello. The shrine of the convent church is particularly well endowed in religious relics and jewels.

Girls wait with mixed emotions for start of film at a Madrid cinema.

From Plaza del Callao, the Gran Vía continues downhill towards the **Plaza de España** through more shopping, strolling and nightlife territory. Two controversial skyscrapers, of 26 and 34 storeys, have changed the atmosphere of the plaza, a sanctuary of grass, flowers, trees and fountains. A favourite sight, especially with visiting photographers, is the Cervantes Monument. A stone sculpture honouring the author looms behind bronze statues of his immortal creations, Don Quixote and Sancho Panza, astride their horse and donkey, respectively.

Calle de la Princesa, which begins at Plaza de España, is actually an extension of the Gran Vía aimed north-west. The house at Calle de la Princesa, 22, is literally palatial; it calls to mind a scaled-down Buckingham Palace. Tucked away in a comfortable park behind high railings, the **Palacio de Liria** is the residence of the Duchess of Alba. The family picture gallery includes works by Rembrandt, Titian, Rubens, Van Dyck, El Greco and Goya. The palace is closed to the public except by special arrangement.

Calle de la Princesa's smart trajectory ends where the University district begins. The landmarks here are the Air Force headquarters (a modern copy of the Escorial) and Madrid's youngest triumphal arch. It commemorates the Franco victory of 1939.

Madrid's Own Words

Sereno. Madrid's night-watchmen used to appear at the clap of the hands to unlock front doors of hotels and apartment houses. Tradition suffered a crushing blow in 1976, when the *serenos* were enlisted as auxiliary police. *Madrileños* now carry their own keys... and secrets.

Tasca. A bar specializing in *tapas,* tasty snacks consumed while standing in a litter of prawn shells and olive stones.

Tertulia. The unofficial club of conversationalists meeting in a café. The tradition is withering as life's pace accelerates.

Tuna. Band of troubadours in medieval costume, usually university students, who serenade clients in bars and restaurants for tips.

Zarzuela. A uniquely Spanish form of operetta, often on themes indigenous to Madrid.

The Prado

Madrid's pride, the Prado Museum, is indisputably the world's greatest collection of Spanish paintings. (Picasso's *Guernica* is in the Prado Annex—Casón del Buen Retiro—see p. 43.) In addition, there are hundreds of famous foreign works.

A serious student of art might well plan an entire Madrid itinerary around repeated visits to the Prado; but the tourist in a rush, trying to include so many highlights, may have to settle for a couple of hours. If the fast visit consists of aimless trudging through nearly 100 rooms, squinting for familiar pictures, the trip could be exhausting and only mildly edifying.

You should, for best results, do some planning. Here is one way out of the labyrinth: a suggested two-hour tour of the top 15 old masters, designed so a visitor can examine the most masterpieces per mile. Unfortunately the Prado is undergoing renovations and many of the pictures described below may have been moved temporarily from their accustomed places. Some of them may not be on view and certain rooms, or even entire wings, may be closed. The **31** museum is open from 9 a.m. to 7 p.m. (2 p.m. on Sunday and some holidays). Closed Monday.

First climb the stairway to the side entrance at the north end of the building (facing Calle de Felipe IV and the Ritz Hotel).

In the main rotunda (Room 1), spare a glance for the sculpture of honour, a bronze by the Italian Leone Leoni showing the Emperor Charles V stamping out the Turkish foe. The emperor's armour is removable; underneath, he's as naked as a Greek god.

Spanish art forms the backbone of the art treasures in store, but since we're near the early Flemish masters, let's turn right and take a brief look into Room 41. Painted in the middle of the 15th century, the *Descent from the Cross* by **Van der Weyden**, with its griefstricken faces, shows unbelievable powers of draughtsmanship.

The Spanish call **Hieronymus Bosch** "El Bosco"—which is the way you will see his works labelled in Rooms 43 and 44. This Dutch genius, portraying the terrors and superstitions of the medieval peasant mind, calls to memory the hallucinations of Salvador Dalí, but Bosch was 400 years ahead of his time. The large triptych called *The Garden of Delights* is the all-time masterpiece of surrealism, full of sensuous fantasies and apocalyptical nightmares.

Sharing space here with his contemporary Bosch, the German painter **Albrecht Dürer** tackles more tangible subjects. His carefully posed self-portrait at the age of 26 shows every ruffle of his shirt and every curl in his flowing hair. He is also represented here by two charming nudes, *Adam* and *Eve*.

Return again across the rotunda to the north-east corner of the main floor, Room 2. **Raphael** (1483–1520) painted the explosive character study called *The Cardinal*. Centuries of investigation have failed to uncover the identity of the subject, with his fishy eyes, aquiline nose and cool, thin lips.

Room 3: In the late 15th century, in Venice, **Antonello da Messina** portrayed *Christ Sustained by an Angel*. With its realistic detail, the whole mood is one of intense sadness. In this room are three great tablets by the Florentine master **Botticelli**. *The Story of Nastagio degli Onesti* illustrates a tale from the *Decameron* of Boccaccio. The

Past Masters of Spanish Painting

In the Prado, the greatest of the great Spanish painters—Goya, El Greco, Murillo and Velázquez—are represented by literally dozens of works, many of them world-famous masterpieces:

Francisco de Goya (1746–1828). A philanderer in his youth, Goya had to flee Saragossa in 1763 for the anonymity of Madrid. He went on to become the king's principal painter. He worked mainly in the neo-Classical manner, and eventually developed a distinctive style that anticipated Impressionism.

El Greco (1541–1614). Born in Crete, resident in Italy, El Greco is a very Spanish painter nonetheless. He worked in Toledo, his adopted city, for 37 years, toiling away at the immense and intensely personal religious canvases that are his hallmark. Asymmetrical compositions, vivid colours and a mood of ecstacy typify his work.

Bartolomé Murillo (1617–1682). An uneven painter, Murillo is, alas, better known for his late pictures in the *estilo vaporoso* (melting style). Ignore the soft-focus and sentimental madonnas and beggar boys and concentrate instead on the naturalistic street urchins and heartfelt religious works.

Diego Velázquez (1599–1660). Apprenticed at age 14 to the Sevillan Pacheco, Velázquez showed his genius early on. A realist approach and virtuoso handling made his reputation. Of his varied output, the portraits stand out for their psychological penetration. Striking too, is the brilliant colour and brushwork that grows ever freer.

---

three panels are a Renaissance storyboard full of colour and action set in an enchanting landscape.

Room 4: *The Annunciation* by **Fra Angelico** is half-way in style between the Middle Ages and the Renaissance. The sunbeam is gold, the columns are graceful and, in the background, Adam and Eve wear robes.

Room 5: **Correggio's** masterpiece, *Noli me tangere,* shows Mary Magdalene awestruck at the sight of the resurrected Christ. The painting pulls the figures out from a lush, forested background.

Rooms 7, 8 and 9: For an artist who painted official portraits and religious works, **Titian** seemed to have no difficulty changing gear to the **33**

downright lascivious. His *Bacanal* may be a reaction to his more serious assignments, but it is about as far as an orgy can go within the bounds of a museum. Two variations on a theme, *Venus Enjoying Herself with Music* and *Venus Enjoying Herself with Love and Music,* maintain the sensuous effect, though by current standards they might be considered as self-parody. Titian's *Portrait of the Emperor Charles V,* on horseback at the Battle of Mühlberg (1547), set the standard for court painters of the next century. While you're enjoying the Prado's splendid Titian collection, don't miss his self-portrait painted at the age of 89. Unlike many of his contemporaries who were doomed to an early death in poverty, this sprightly Venetian is reputed to have lived to 98.

Our route passes through Room 11, where you can get a glimpse of the experiments in light and shade of the devout Spanish painter, **Francisco de Zurbarán.**

Rooms 9B and 10B: El Greco enthusiasts will want to take a trip to Toledo for the fullest view of his works, but the Prado displays a good cross-section. Here is *Knight with Hand on Chest,* the distinguished *caballero* all in black, signed in Greek capital letters "Domenikos Theotokopoulos", the artist's real name. Another signed painting is a delicate portrait of St. Mary. The large painting, *Adoration of the Shepherds,* is a prime example of El Greco's unique

Left: still life outside the Prado. Detail from the fantasy Garden of Delights by Dutch master Bosch.

lighting effects. In addition, there are pictures of the apostles, saints and other religious subjects, a two-room survey of the mystical and passionately coloured world of the 16th-century genius.

Continue now through the main hall (Rooms 26 and 27) and turn left in the very centre of the building: Room 12 is the place of honour of one of the finest Spanish artists, **Diego Velázquez.** Here are paintings of the high and the mighty along with studies of fun-loving ordinary mortals. As court painter to Philip IV, Velázquez was obliged to devote most of his time to official portraits. But he enlivened his subjects with almost impressionistic brushwork and colour, and his landscapes and skies are exquisite. One of the Prado's most-discussed works is his *Surrender of Breda,* commemorating a Spanish victory over Dutch forces in 1625. The chivalry of the winning general, the exhaustion of the loser, the less disguised emotions of their retinues, the extraordinary array of upraised lances

Salmer, Barcelona

of the Spaniards and the burning landscape show us Velázquez at his most profound. More Velázquez—princes and princesses, plus freaks and saints—are hung in Rooms 13 and 14, leading to the climax with Spain's all-time favourite painting. It has a room to itself, Room 15. *Las Meninas* (The Maids of Honour) is the triumph of Velázquez over light and space. You could spend an hour trying to determine how he managed to create the illusion of three dimensions. (A large mirror has been placed in the back of the room to help you study the depth factor.) But apart from the tricks, this giant canvas is a delight in itself and a crowning achievement of the artist, who painted himself with palette in hand at the left side of his own masterpiece.

The layout of the museum suggests a change now to Flemish and Dutch painters before returning to the art of Spain. Actually, there is a Spanish connection. **Peter Paul Rubens,** whose pictures are shown in Rooms 16 to 20, came to Spain twice and met Velázquez. His noble ancestry enabled him to follow a career as a diplomat as well as an artist. The Prado is well endowed with the works of Rubens on

biblical and mythological themes, as well as royal portraits. Outstanding here is the huge *Adoration of the Magi,* as well as a painting of a radically different type, *The Three Graces.* Three fleshy nudes are shown in an equally lush landscape; the blonde on the left is said to be Rubens's second wife, Helena.

Room 23: **Rembrandt** is represented in the Prado by only two paintings. *Artemis* was signed by the newly wed artist in 1634. The self-portrait of an older Rembrandt is the familiar broad face glowing from a dark-brown background.

From Rembrandt, follow the corridor labelled Room 31 to the large hall (32) dedicated to **Francisco de Goya.** In the year 1786, he became an official painter to the Spanish court. *The Family of Charles IV,* his most celebrated royal portrait, is daringly frank. Only the royal children look anything like attractive; the adults presumably are true-to-life. The lady with head averted represented a not-yet-announced in-law. Taking a leaf from Velázquez, Goya stations himself on the left side of this painting.

To continue the Prado's survey of Goya, you'll have to

Spain's favourite painting, Las Meninas, *is a triumph of illusionism.*

go out into the main corridor (Rooms 29 and 28) and then down the stairs (called Room 45) to the ground floor. In its abstruse way, the route passes through Room 59 and the passageway numbered 58 to a gratifyingly large wing (Rooms 53 to 57A) devoted to Goya.

One of history's great protest pictures, *The Executions of the 3rd of May,* shows the shooting of Spanish patriots in 1808 by the French. Goya witnessed this tragedy of the War of Independence from the window of his cottage, then went to the scene by moonlight to sketch the victims.

Nothing in life escaped him—honour and joy, city **37**

Goya's scandalous Naked Maja *still draws curious crowds in the Prado.*

and country, kings and peasants, disasters and cruelty, all recorded with compassion and colour, and on occasion boisterous good humour. Of all Goya's paintings—in fact of all the paintings in the Prado—none is more discussed and disputed than *The Naked Maja* (Room 57A). Nudes had been almost nonexistent in Spanish painting, and the principal gossip for over 160 years has concerned the identity of the model. The face is awkwardly superimposed on the body, suggesting that the lady was thus disguised. Rumours of a scandalous affair between Goya and the Duchess of Alba are always mentioned in this context and always denied. The other half of the famous pair is *The Clothed Maja,* the same lady provocatively robed.

So much for the scandalous. Now roam around the Goya rooms at will, to see how the people of Madrid lived at the end of the 18th century. Look at his sketches, engravings, cartoons for tapestries, and finally the "Black Paintings" of his last phase—the mad murals Goya produced in the bitterness of old age and deafness. His visions of death and monsters are a long way from the innocence of his lively sketches of children's games, but they all made up his prolific and impassioned reportage of life itself.

For your next visit to the Prado, make amends to some of those regretfully overlooked: Brueghel, Caravaggio, Coello, David, Van Dyck, Gainsborough, Herrera, Mengs, Murillo, Reynolds, Ribera, Teniers, Tiepolo and Watteau. Then return to your favourite pictures by the three greatest Spaniards, El Greco, Velázquez and Goya.

Missing Masters
Fate and turbulent times dealt unkindly with the last remains of Spain's three greatest painters.

El Greco died in Toledo in 1614. He was buried in a local church, but the coffin was transferred to another, which was destroyed. His bones were never found.

Velázquez (died in 1660) was entombed in a Madrid parish church which was demolished; the remains were lost.

Goya died in 1828 in Bordeaux, France, where he was interred. In 1899, the remains were sent back to Spain, but the skull was missing.

Other Museums and Sights

Royal Palace
(Palacio Real)

Soon after the coronation of King Juan Carlos I in 1975, official tour guides noticed a distinct increase in the number of visitors to Madrid's Royal Palace. No wonder: a worked-in palace is much more interesting than a historical relic. But there's a disadvantage. Certain days of the week, not always predictable, the palace is closed to the public for official functions. Ask at the tourist office for the schedule.

The Royal Palace is often called El Palacio de Oriente (Palace of the East) in spite of its westerly location. It is set among formal gardens on a bluff overlooking the Manzanares Valley. The old Moorish fortress on the site burned down in 1734, whereupon King Philip V ordered the construction of an immense new palace in French style. His command produced this imperious residence, loaded with art and history.

For security reasons, visitors are forbidden to wander on their own, but are escorted in groups according to language. The basic one-hour tour takes in only a fraction of the 2,000 rooms. It begins with the climb up the main staircase—bright, airy and ceremonious beneath an arched ceiling. Each step is a single slab of marble. The marble lions on the bannisters don't match; one is French, the other Spanish.

The apartments of Charles III consist of one lavish room after another. The outstanding **Gasparini Room** is named after the artist (Matias Gasparini of Naples) who mobilized stone-cutters, sculptors, glass-blowers, clock-makers, silver-smiths, cabinet-makers and embroiderers to produce this example of Rococo at its most overwhelming. Floor, walls and ceiling swirl with special effects.

The **Ceremonial Dining Room,** seating 145 guests, was built for the wedding of Alfonso XII and his second wife, Maria Christina, in 1879. Do notice the 15 chandeliers, ten candelabra and 18th-century Chinese porcelain jars along walls hung with Brussels tapestries.

The so-called **Official Chamber,** all red velvet and gold, is still used when ambassadors come to present credentials. The **Throne Room** occupies the very centre of the south façade of the palace. Red velvet and mirrors in matching gilt frames cover the walls. The ceiling, painted by Tiepolo in 1764, aims to depict "the greatness of the Spanish monarchy with its provinces and states". Four gilded bronze lions defend the throne.

For a basic fee, you can see all the sights on the standard tour. An extra charge is made for additional sights within the palace:

The Crown Jewels. Dramatically displayed behind glass in a modern vault, an impressive collection of sceptres, crowns, jewels and relics.

Museum of Paintings. They go back to religious works which belonged to Queen Isabella I. In the room dedicated to Velázquez, note the large painting of a rearing, riderless horse; the artist died before he could paint in the royal horseman. Works by Zurbarán, El Greco and Goya round out the collection.

Scene of regal ceremonies and portentous events: Royal Palace as viewed under a typical Madrid sky.

Hall of the Halberdiers. Mostly ancient Flemish and Spanish tapestries in a remarkable state of preservation, the colours still rich.

Royal Library. Twenty-four rooms containing 300,000 works—rare editions, manuscripts and maps. Valuable musical instruments on show include two violins by Stradivarius, kept under glass but tuned and played periodically.

Royal Pharmacy. With a re-creation of a 17th-century alchemist's distillation room. Cupboards lining two rooms are filled with matching glass and porcelain apothecary jars specially ordered by Charles IV in 1794.

Royal Armoury. If the children—or anyone else for that matter—have begun to droop from all the mileage, the art and the history, this should perk them up. Swashbuckling swordsmen and jousting horsemen are commemorated here in a display of authentic battle flags, trophies, shields and weapons. The armoury is officially called the finest collection of its type in the world.

More for Art Lovers
Private collections, state-run galleries and religious institutions add to Madrid's renown as an art centre. Almost all

Miró and other moderns of Spain cheer Contemporary Art Museum.

museums are open from about 10 a.m. to 2 p.m.; for specific hours, see p. 114.

In nearly all of the Madrid museums, the legends are in Spanish only. Hint: *Siglo III a. C.* = 3rd century B.C. *Siglo III d. C.* = 3rd century A.D.

Museo Lázaro Galdiano, Calle de Serrano, 122. An astonishingly wide-ranging and priceless private collection bequeathed to the nation. Ancient jewellery including a Celtic diadem from the 2nd century B.C. Medieval and Renaissance masterpieces in ivory and enamel, gold and silver. Rare church vestments, medieval weapons. Paintings: a Rembrandt portrait of Saskia van Uylenburgh, dated the year they were married. *Vision of Tondal* is Hieronymus Bosch at his most diabolical. Goya: a rich repository of official portraits, colourful sketches of real life, and haunting scenes of witches and horrors. El Greco: a sensitive *St. Francis of Assisi* and an early (1562) picture from his Venetian period; English painters: Reynolds, Gainsborough and Constable, and an unexpected entry by the American Gilbert Stuart. But the museum's greatest pride, spotlighted in its own niche on the ground floor, is a portrait of angelic beauty, painted around 1480 by Leonardo da Vinci, entitled *The Saviour*.

Casón del Buen Retiro (Prado Annex), Calle de Felipe IV. Awkwardly subtitled "Section of 19th-Century Spanish Art of the Prado" and housed in a gravely colonnaded palace.

Picasso's *Guernica*, now back after 44 years in New York, is undoubtedly the star of the show. Apart from that, more Goya: paintings of death and daily life. Portraits, frequently unflattering, by Vicente López (Goya's prize pupil). A hall of historical paintings, strong on melodrama, blood and Spanish honour. And on to early Spanish impressionists.

Museo Sorolla, Paseo del General Martínez Campos, 37. The only Madrid museum devoted to a single painter, this mansion was the home and studio of Joaquín Sorolla (1863–1923). Close to 300 paintings on view, showing the Valencian impressionist's areas of immense talent—seaside scenes and landscapes.

Museo de Arte Contemporáneo (Museum of Contemporary Art), Avenida de Juan de Herrera, Ciudad Universitaria. This starkly modern museum is warm and attractive inside a somewhat forbid- **43**

ding skyscraper. Beautifully arranged and documented displays from early 20th-century realism to post-pop art. Picasso, Miró and Dalí, of course, plus many talented Spanish artists of lesser fame. First-class sculpture throughout and in the surrounding gardens.

Museo Cerralbo, Calle de Ventura Rodríguez, 17. Another nobleman's collection bequeathed to his country. It's more like visiting an art collector's house than a museum; few works are identified or marked. But there are paintings by El Greco, Murillo, Ribera, Zurbarán, Titian and Caravaggio. The mansion's split-level library would make any bibliophile jealous.

Convento de la Encarnación (Convent of the Incarnation), Plaza de la Encarnación. Founded in 1611 by Margaret of Austria, this convent-church-museum has accumulated an interesting art collection. Hundreds of religious relics. In the 18th-century Baroque church, you may hear the nuns praying, but you'll never see them; they are cloistered on the other side of the grillwork.

Panteón de Goya—Ermita de San Antonio de la Florida, Paseo de la Florida. In an unglamorous area between the railway yards and the river, Goya's greatest fresco covers the cupola of an 18th-century chapel. Four large mirrors, arrayed at crucial points to permit detailed scrutiny, allow you to study the painting without straining your neck. An identical chapel has been built alongside this one so that the local congregation is no longer bothered by tourists paying homage to Goya. His tomb was installed here in 1919.

Understanding the Past

Museo Arqueológico, Calle de Serrano, 13. Emphasizing the art of the ancient inhabitants of Spain. Charming statuettes and jewelry belonging to the 2nd-century B.C. Carthaginian settlers of the island of Ibiza. Miraculously preserved mosaics from 2nd-century A.D. Roman Spain. An unforgettable item, *La Dama de Elche* (The Lady of Elche), a stone sculpture found in Alicante Province in 1897. This thoroughly noble goddess, with beautiful cheekbones, lips and eyes, wearing a fanciful headdress, may be 2,500 years old. Items from the more recent past cover Visigothic religious works and the intricacies of Muslim Spanish workmanship.

On the museum grounds —or, more correctly, *under* the ground—they have reproduced the painted scenes discovered in a cave in Altamira, in northern Spain: prehistoric paintings of animals, dating back perhaps 15,000 years and representing man's first illustrations of the world around him. A facsimile especially worth seeing now that the caves are closed to visitors.

A pre-Columbian figure from Costa Rica on view at Museum of America.

Museo de América (closed for renovation), Avenida de los Reyes Católicos, 6 (Ciudad Universitaria). To Spaniards, "America" means Central and South America. Peru and Mexico provided outstanding pre-Columbian statues and artefacts. Two rare Mayan manuscripts (codices) are displayed in their entirety under glass—mysterious symbols and delightful illustrations which have long fascinated scholars.

Templo Egipcio de Debod. Threatened with submersion during the building of the Aswan High Dam, this 25-century-old Egyptian temple was dismantled and shipped to Madrid, stone by stone. It has been reconstructed amidst palm trees and other alien flora in the gardens of the Cuartel de la Montaña. The sight *from* the temple is also something special: a panoramic view over Madrid.

Arts and Crafts

Museo Nacional de Artes Decorativas, Calle de Montalbán, 12. Full of the things antique collectors dream of finding at the flea market *(Rastro)*—but here they are real. The best of old Spanish glassware, woodwork, tapestry, porcelain, jewelry.

Museo Romántico, Calle de San Mateo, 13. Spaniards seem incurably nostalgic for the age of love seats, Rococo mirrors and petticoated young **45**

princesses. Among the whimsical 19th-century relics are some genuinely interesting works of art.

Real Fábrica de Tapices (Royal Tapestry Factory), Calle de Fuenterrabía, 2. All that has changed since Philip V founded this workshop in 1721 is the method of dyeing the wool. Goya worked here, creating the designs on which tapestries were based. They are still being copied, along with contemporary designs, on commission.

Just for Curiosity

Museo de Carruajes (Carriage Museum), Campo del Moro. This installation, on the far side of the Royal Palace, houses royal transport of all kinds up to the eve of the age of automobiles. See a 16th-century litter thought to have borne the Emperor Charles V when he was suffering from gout. Much more recent history was made by the gala coach of Alfonso XIII, still showing signs of damage from a 1906 assassination plot. Here are coaches with the evocative Spanish names *berlina, lando, vis-a-vis, faeton* and *milord*. A stage-coach, ancient sedan chairs, sleds and saddles round off the well-organized curiosities.

Fábrica Nacional de Moneda y Timbre (also known as Casa de la Moneda, or Mint Museum), Paseo del Doctor Esquerdo, 36. A modern, attractive money museum on the top floor of the actual mint. While you explore the 22 halls with 25,000 numismatic exhibits, you can actually thrill to the vibration of the great presses downstairs manufacturing pesetas. Among the oddities on view: a 12th-century Chinese banknote, early American dollars and a proliferation of Russian banknotes issued in the confusion of the revolutionary period.

Museo Colón de Figuras de Cera (Wax Museum), Plaza de Colón. Privately run collection of realistic wax figures representing historical and contemporary celebrities, with special audiovisual effects.

Museo Naval, Calle de Montalbán, 2. Inside the Navy headquarters, this museum reflects the old glory of Spanish seamen—explorers and their ships. A treasure here, a map dating from 1500, discloses a startling amount of knowledge about the newly discovered western hemisphere.

Museo Municipal (Municipal Museum), Calle de

Fuencarral, 78. The best part is the exterior of the building, built by Pedro Ribera in the mid-18th century. The memorably ornamental portal is the last word in Rococo pomp.

Museo Taurino (Bullfighting Museum), part of Plaza de Toros Monumental de Las Ventas (bullring). Historic posters, capes, swords, paintings and photos for *aficionados* of the *corrida*.

Cervantes waits for inspiration at his desk in Wax Museum display.

Landmarks and Parks

Paseo de la Castellana, Madrid's principal north-south avenue, runs for several miles through the heart of the city. Heading northwards from Plaza de Colón, you come to a newer section of town. Patrician town-houses in the central area give way to luxurious modern apartment blocks with landscaped balconies.

Nuevos Ministerios (New Ministries). A bureaucrat's dream along Paseo de la Castellana, this mammoth 20th-century project dignifies the Ministries of Housing, Labour and Public Works, reminiscent of Washington, D.C.

Once a royal forest, Casa de Campo now has public lake, zoo, funfair.

Plaza de Colón. Separating La Castellana from the Paseo Recoletos is a wide-open space that has been the recent scene of far-reaching public-works projects. The city airline terminal operates below ground, far beneath an 1885 statue of Christopher Columbus and a monument to the
discovery of the New World.

There is also the Centro Cultural de la Villa (City Cultural Center), with facilities for concerts, theatre, art exhibitions and films.

Puerta de Alcalá. This super-monumental triumphal arch, surmounted by warrior-angels, honours Charles III. Until the late 19th century, this was the very edge of town. Now the Plaza de la Independencia, in which the arch stands, is a bedlam of midtown traffic.

One of a dozen entrances to **Parque del Retiro** faces Plaza de la Independencia. Until little over a century ago, the Retiro was a royal preserve. Now it's the easiest place for *Madrileños* to take a family outing (see page 91).

Another central breathing space, the **Real Jardín Botánico** (Royal Botanical Garden) adjacent to the Prado, was founded two centuries ago. It is packed with enlightening displays of flowers and plants from many regions.

Las Cortes Españolas, the Spanish Parliament, occupies a mid-19th-century building very near the Prado Museum. Before the Corinthian columns stand two ornamental lions, cast from the metal of guns captured from some of Spain's 19th-century enemies.

The **Puente de Segovia** (Segovia Bridge), Madrid's oldest bridge, dates from 1584. Juan de Herrera, the man who built the Escorial, designed this sturdy, granite span. It crosses Madrid's very own river, the Manzanares, a trickle of a river, no competition for the Mississippi, the Amazon or even the Thames. As Lope de Vega wrote, *"Tenéis un hermoso puente con esperanzas de río".* ("You have a fine bridge, with hopes for a river.")

Ciudad Universitaria, the University City, was built on the ruins of the district that suffered the worst damage in the Civil War.

A drive around indicates the ambitious expanse of the campus and the mixture of architectural styles.

Parque Casa de Campo. Another former royal preserve, forested by Philip II in 1559. It is reachable by bus, suburban railway line or cable car *(teleférico).* Thousands of acres of woodland interspersed with attractions and amenities. Hire a boat on the park lake. Swim in the pool. Practice bull-fighting. Ride the Ferris wheel and eat toffee-apples at the funfair. See the modern (1972) zoo, where 150 kinds of animals show off behind moats, not bars.

Excursions

Toledo

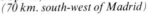

Pop. 45,000
(70 km. south-west of Madrid)

All of Spain—tradition, grandeur and art—is crammed into this small city set on a Castilian hilltop. This one-time imperial capital remains the religious centre of Spain and an incomparable treasure-house of the fine arts. You may get lost exploring the back streets, little changed over the centuries, but you'll never forget the aesthetic adventure.

If you see only one Spanish city outside Madrid, make it Toledo. And if you visit only one church in all Spain, make it the **Cathedral of Toledo.** You can locate the cathedral from any part of town, thanks to its Gothic tower, topped by a spire strangely ringed by spikes. But at ground level, the building is hemmed in by Toledo's clutter of back streets, so you cannot obtain a sufficiently dramatic view from any vantage point. No matter; the glory of this church can be seen inside it—the stained glass, wrought iron, sculpture and painting produced by platoons of geniuses.

49

Toledo's eminence as the centre of Christian Spain goes back to the first synods and ecclesiastical councils, held there as early as the year 400. But with the Muslim invasion of Spain in 711, Christianity went underground. After the reconquest of Toledo in 1085, with the legendary warrior El Cid leading the way, mosques were turned into churches. In 1222, funds were appropriated for a fitting cathedral. The construction lasted two and a half centuries; the ornamentation took longer.

In the centre of the five-aisled Gothic basilica, the **coro** (choir) is a marvel of wood-carving. Illustrations of the Christian triumph at Granada in 1492, on the lower choir stalls, were created by Rodrigo Alemán only three years after the great event itself. The higher stalls came later, carved by the Renaissance masters Alonso Berruguete (left) and Felipe Bigarny. The 13th- or 14th-century statue known as *The White Virgin* is believed to be French. Notice her smile.

Across the transept, the **main altar** outdoes the coro's considerable splendour. A magnificent polychrome retable tells New Testament stories in fervent detail, rising in five tiers. Immeasurable talent and toil went into this masterpiece of teamwork.

Just behind the back wall of the main chapel, the **Transparente** is the cathedral's most unforgettable innovation. Although the work is fantastically elaborate, it was done by one man. Narciso Tomé took all the credit as architect, sculptor and painter. What this 18th-century artist did was to open the ceiling and draw heavenly light into the sanctuary, at the same time leading our eyes up to an amazing launching pad for the soul. While the cathedral's 750 stained-glass windows illuminate with sublime restraint, Tomé's bronze, marble and jasper ensemble of colour, shape and symbolism startles as it inspires.

The **Sala Capitular** (Chapter-House) is a strangely oriental room with an intricate ceiling in the style called *mudéjar* (the work of Christianized Muslims after the Reconquest). Around the walls are portraits of the archbishops of Toledo, starting with St. Eugene (A.D. 96) and featuring Cardinal Cisneros, who ordered the construction of this hall.

In the **Tesoro** (Treasury Room), reliquaries, chalices and crowns take second place

to the lavish monstrance (also ordered by Cisneros). This towering vessel, made of 5,600 individual parts, was the work of the German silversmith Enrique de Arfe (Heinrich von Harff). It was subsequently gilded. Precious stones add to the glitter. The monstrance is said to weigh 17 *arrobas* (over 440 pounds).

The **sacristy** is a museum of art, air-conditioned for the sake of the paintings, not the people. The pictures are clearly labelled (a rarity in Spanish churches), so you won't have to keep asking, "Could this really be another genuine El Greco?" It certainly could. In all, there are 16 of them in this small collection. In addition to portraits of the Virgin, Christ with the Cross, and the apostles, there is a large and outstanding El Greco work over the main altar of the sacristy—*Expolio* (The Saviour Stripped of His Raiment). The museum also displays first-rate paintings by Goya, Titian and Velázquez.

Tourists are charged a fee

Among Toledo's glories: main altar of cathedral has splendid retable.

for admission to closed areas of the cathedral, such as the choir, treasury and museum.

The cathedral's only competitor for domination of the Toledo skyline is the **Alcázar,** a fortress destroyed and rebuilt many times. It began as a Roman redoubt, but its present style was devised in the 16th century. Since then it has been used as a royal palace, army post, school and prison. During the Spanish Civil War, it was a stronghold of the pro-Franco forces, who held out during a 72-day siege which all but destroyed the Alcázar. The Nationalist commandant, Colonel José Moscardó Ituarte, received a telephone call from the enemy announcing that his son, held hostage, would be executed unless the fortress surrendered. In a supremely Spanish reply, the colonel advised his son to "pray, shout *'Viva España'* and die like a hero". More than a month after the son was killed, the siege was lifted. You can visit the shrapnel-scarred office of the unyielding colonel and see other relics of the drama—an ancient Swedish radio transmitter, bound copies of the *Illustrated London News* riddled with bullet holes, two vintage Harley-Davidson motorcycles, the primitive underground hospital and the small, dark room in which two babies were born while the fighting raged.

The triangular-shaped main plaza of Toledo has also been rebuilt after Civil War destruction. The **Plaza de Zocodover** is where the Moorish market *(zoco)* was held in the Middle Ages. It was also the scene of the great fiestas, tournaments and executions of criminals and infidels. Suggestively, the horseshoe arch leading from the square towards the river is called El Arco de la Sangre (Arch of Blood).

Just down the hill beyond the arch in Calle de Cervantes, the 16th-century **Hospital de la Santa Cruz** (Hospital of the Holy Cross), now a museum, maintains a most elaborate façade. The main portal is of stone carved in the style called Plateresque, because it seems as delicate as a silversmith's work (*platero* means silversmith). Inside, great wooden ceilings add to a feeling of opulent spaciousness. The provincial archaeological museum is housed here, but greater interest accrues to the art collection. Here, too, El Greco fans are in for a happy surprise—a wide selection of his works, highlighted by the **53**

TOLEDO

Altarpiece of the Assumption, painted just a year before the artist's death.

At the bottom of Calle de Cervantes is the Paseo del Carmen, a promenade on a bluff overlooking the River Tagus, which flows all the way to Lisbon. From here, you get a fine view of the Bridge of Alcántara, with elements built in the 9th and 13th centuries. And across the river, the Castle of San Servando—originally a monastery, then a medieval fortress, designed to defend Toledo from any attack from the east. While the bridge, the fortress and other monuments are carefully preserved, the authorities have been unable to defend the Tagus from industrial pollution and detergent foam.

Every Tuesday, the Paseo del Carmen is the site of the big outdoor **market.** Here you can spy on the shouting, shoving and colour of unselfconscious provincial Spain. The street market caters to practical local needs—basic clothing and household goods. For tourist requirements, you'll have to try the shops elsewhere in Toledo. They sell swords, of course—bullfighter models or miniatures for letter openers, or historic reproductions. You can watch the artisans making a variety of damascene items. The ceramics are inventive. Or you might like to own an old-fashioned illustrated lady's folding fan.

The **Parish Church of Santo Tomé** is a landmark because of its stately *mudéjar* tower. Here they charge a fee for the sight of a single picture. But what a painting! El Greco's *Burial of the Count of Orgaz* manages to combine in a magic fusion the mundane and the spiritual. It depicts grave-faced local noblemen attending the count's funeral (which occurred nearly three centuries before the picture was painted). Tradition says two saints made an appearance at the funeral. El Greco shows St. Augustine and St. Stephen, in splendid ecclesiastical garb, lifting the count's body. Above, angels and saints crowd the clouds. The whole story is told in perfect pictorial balance and with El Greco's unpredictable colours.

Toledo was El Greco's adopted home town, where he spent the most productive years of his prolific career. Just down the hill from Santo Tomé, a house in which he may have lived has been reconstructed and linked to a museum dedicated to the painter. The authentic 16th- **55** century furnishings and a tranquil garden assist the mood. Several of the master's paintings are on display, among them *A View and Map of Toledo,* showing how little the city has changed since his day. Dramatically displayed on an easel stands his *Portrait of St. Peter.*

The **El Greco House** was originally built by Samuel Levi, a remarkable 14th-century Jewish financier and friend of King Peter I of Castile. Since the 12th century, Toledo had been a centre of Jewish poets, historians and philosophers. Jews, Arabs and Benedictine monks worked together in translation teams. As Europe awakened from the Dark Ages, Toledo provided a key link in the transmission of vital knowledge of Arabic science and Greek philosophy to the Western world.

During those halcyon days, Samuel Levi, as devout as he was rich, built a synagogue next to his home. It now bears the curious name of **La Sinagoga del Tránsito** (Synagogue of the Dormition). Muslim artists created a ceiling of cedar imported from Lebanon; they adorned the walls with filigrees intricate beyond belief, as well as inscriptions in Hebrew from the Psalms.

Upstairs, a large gallery was reserved for the women of the congregation. You may be surprised to find Christian tombstones in the floor. After the expulsion of the Jews from Spain, the synagogue was converted into a church. Nowadays, the **Sephardi Museum** is attached to Samuel Levi's synagogue, with exhibits of medieval tombs, scrolls and vestments.

Like the Tránsito, **La Sinagoga de Santa María la Blanca** (St. Mary the White) received its present name after its conversion to a church. No signs of the Jewish presence remain, yet this five-aisled building, with its 24 columns supporting horseshoe arches, was the main synagogue of 12th-century Toledo. Constructed by Muslim artisans, it looks more like a mosque than a synagogue or church. In the 15th century, bloodthirsty mobs raided the synagogue and massacred the Jewish population. After the pogrom, the old structure served a bizarre variety of purposes —as Catholic chapel, con-

Toledo skyline is almost unchanged since days of El Greco. So are the laundry methods in rural Castile.

vent for "fallen" women, army barracks and quartermaster's depot. This now empty building evokes the most dramatic memories.

A final church of Toledo, with regal connections: Ferdinand and Isabella built **San Juan de los Reyes** (St. John of the Kings) out of their private fortune in commemoration of the 1476 victory over the Portuguese in the Battle of Toro. The architectural style is a combination of Gothic, Renaissance and *mudéjar* elements. Look for a poignant souvenir on the outer wall—the chains which held Christian prisoners of the Moors. The cloister here is a superb double-decker of mostly late Gothic style, with elaborate stone carvings; a delightfully placid spot.

On the way out of town, between the 16th-century gateway called La Puerta Nueva de Bisagra and the bullring, there stands the **Hospital de Tavera,** part-palace, part-orphanage, part-church, built by a 16th-century Archbishop of Toledo, Juan Pardo de Tavera. The library contains fascinating old books as well as the bound volumes of the hospital's financial accounts, which record in meticulous script expenditures for fish and chocolate. In the dining room hangs a portrait by Titian of the Emperor Charles V and a painting of the Princess Clara Eugenia by Claudio Coello. Elsewhere in the palace, perhaps inevitably, El Greco is strongly represented. His portrait of the Virgin is stirringly beautiful; his *Baptism of Christ* is one of the artist's last works. A curiosity here is Ribera's portrait of a bearded woman. Notice, too, a small statue of

Two-storey cloister of San Juan de los Reyes is another gem of Toledo.

Christ resurrected, an experiment in sculpture by the great El Greco.

If you're driving back to Madrid from Toledo and would like a brief halt almost exactly mid-way, the village of **Illescas** (33 km. from Toledo) holds a surprise in store for you. Few visitors discover the village or its **Hospital de la Virgen de la Caridad** (Convent of the Virgin of Charity), in whose church hang five El Grecos. The locals seem only mildly interested in the artistic treasure in their midst. They tend to prefer another picture on display—a straightforward painting of the church itself.

Near Toledo, a bicyclist tilts his imagination at Castilian windmills.

Segovia

Pop. 40,000
(88 km. north-west of Madrid)

The delights of Segovia rise up unexpectedly on all sides. Before you have time to digest the glory of the natural setting, the magnificent skyline will have captivated you. Then, just when this mirage of medieval Spain comes into focus, your attention is drawn to some equally breathtaking monument or building. These **59** are wonders to be savoured one at a time.

First, the site. Segovia juts out from the clean-air plateau in the heart of Old Castile. This is pure Castilian country—wide-open spaces made for cavaliers, interrupted only occasionally by a clump of trees, a lonely farmhouse, a monastery or a castle. The Sierra de Guadarrama, where you can ski in the winter, fills half the horizon.

Segovia's three greatest monuments are—in chronological order—the aqueduct, the Alcázar and the cathedral.

The **Roman aqueduct,** a work of art and a triumph of engineering, marches right through the centre of town. Looked at from our era of instant obsolescence, the builders of this public-works project merit special admiration. The aqueduct is composed of thousands of granite blocks arranged in graceful arches, sometimes two-tiered. It is nearly half a mile long and as much as 150 feet high. This is the last lap of a conduit bringing water from a mountain stream to the walled city. Almost as astonishing as the engineering achievement is the fact the aqueduct has been in constant use not just for 100 years, but 100 generations!

Only a couple of details have been changed. A modern pipeline has been installed in the channel atop the aqueduct; and in the 16th century, a statue of Hercules in a niche over the tallest arch was replaced by a Christian image. Nearly 2,000 years after the aqueduct was finished, it still brings water to Segovia.

The **Alcázar,** Segovia's incomparable royal castle, was built in the most natural strategic spot. It dominates a ridge overlooking the confluence of two rivers, with an unimpeded view of the plateau in all directions. The Romans are thought to have been among the first to build a watchtower here. The present storybook castle is a far cry from the simple stone fortress which took shape in the 12th century. As it grew bigger and more luxurious, it played a more significant historical role. By the 13th century, parliaments were convened here. In 1474, Princess Isabella stayed in the Alcázar at the time of her coronation as Queen of Castile. Here in 1570, King Philip II married his fourth bride, Anne of Austria. Less ceremoniously, the Tower of King John II became a dungeon for 16th-century political prisoners. The most fanciful,

photogenic parts of the castle's superstructure are the work of restoration after a disastrous fire in 1862.

You can sit quietly on a bench in the small park facing the turreted tower and allow the spectacle to sink in. Then cross the drawbridge over the moat and tour the royal rooms, carefully restored with period furnishings. See the Throne Room, the Pinecone Room (named after the designs carved in the ceiling),

Fairy-tale silhouette of Segovia's royal castle. Below: a view from 12th-century St. Martin's Church.

the royal bedrooms, the chapel. In the armoury, see early mortars and cannons, and even earlier lances and crossbows. The view from the open terrace is fit for a king.

From whatever part of town you look at it, the **cathedral** presents a reassuringly beautiful sight. Its pinnacles and cupolas seem to belong to a whole complex of churches, but, in fact, it's all a single elegant monument. Begun in 1525 (but not consecrated until 1768), this is the last of the great Spanish Gothic cathedrals. Its grace and style have won it the nickname of Queen of Cathedrals. Incidentally, the "Queen" was even taller until a lightning bolt lopped off the main tower in 1614. The reconstruction plan warily lowered the profile more than 10 per cent.

Inside, the cathedral's majestic columns and arches are lit by fine stained-glass windows. You will be struck by the sight of two 18th-century organs in all their massive flamboyance. Less obvious are the altarpieces in the chapels, the most important element of which (just to the right of the entrance) is a 16th-century polychrome pietà by the Valencian Juan de Juni.

Alongside the cathedral, delicate arches line the cloister. Admirable but invisible here is a background of persistent and meticulous handiwork. This cloister belonged to the former cathedral which was destroyed; it was moved here, stone by stone, in the 16th century and put back together.

The adjacent museum and chapter-house contain the religious art and relics that one would expect—but with a few surprises. The tapestries are 17th-century Gobelins. On show is the Baroque carriage propelled through the streets of Segovia every Corpus Christi, with its huge 17th-century silver monstrance. Here also is the pathetic reminder of a 14th-century tragedy: the tomb of the infant Prince Pedro, son of Enrique II. He slipped from the arms of his nurse as she admired the view from an open window of the Alcázar. The nanny scarcely hesitated before she leaped after him to death in the moat below.

Only a few streets away to the east, a much older church than the cathedral graces Segovia's most charming square. **St. Martin's Church** is a 12th-century Romanesque beauty with glorious **63** portals and porches. Notice the ingeniously carved stone figures atop the pillars. Plaza de San Martín, which slopes down to Calle de Juan Bravo, is surrounded by noble mansions of the distinct Segovia style. As for Juan Bravo himself, whose flag-waving statue looms here, he defied the Emperor Charles V in the 16th century. Bravo of Segovia and Juan de Padilla of Toledo led an insurrection against absentee rulers and crushing taxes. The so-called *Comunero* movement eventually fizzled out, and both the leaders of the conspiracy were executed; but the brave Bravo is remembered here as the top local hero.

On the subject of statues, notice the primitive sculptures in the square. They may resemble James Thurber's hippopotami, but they are really a legacy of the Celtiberians, who preceded the Romans in ancient Old Castile.

Next to the church, the prison-like building with those fierce, barred windows was, in fact, a prison when it was built in the 17th century. Now it houses a library and archives. Here and throughout the city, the façades of the buildings are subject to elaborate three-dimensional decoration, mainly with geometric forms. The most extreme example, the nearby Casa de los Picos, simply bristles with pointed protuberances.

The main square of Segovia, the **Plaza Mayor,** combines history with real-life bustle. Buildings as pleasing as the 17th-century Town Hall face the large oblong plaza where shoppers, businessmen and tourists take time out for coffee in the fresh air. At festival times, the square is where all the excitement and colour begin.

Total tranquillity permeates the **Monastery of El Parral,** founded in the mid-15th century, lying beyond the city walls, but within easy reach of the centre of town. The architectural details, including a Gothic cloister, are being restored in fits and starts. Especially dramatic is the 16th-century high retable in the monastery's church.

Finally, you should see, just outside the wall and almost in the shadow of the Alcázar, the **Vera Cruz Church,** an unusual 12-sided building, dating from the early 13th century. The Knights of the Holy Sepulchre held court in its unique double-decker chapel surrounded by a circular nave. The Maltese Order, owner of the church for centuries, renovated it in the 1950s. It's still moody.

So much of Segovia is superlative that the 11th-century city wall itself is almost relegated to second-class status. But it's all relative. The mile and a half of wall tends to be irregular, but evocative; here and there you'll come across some warlike, fierce stretches, but mostly the wall is homely and lived-in.

Avila dignitaries lead procession in commemoration of St. Theresa.

Avila

Pop. 32,000
(112 km. north-west of Madrid)

The fairy-tale stone **walls** protecting Avila are just too perfect: they make the city look like a Castilian Disneyland. But they were built in all seriousness in the last decade of the 11th century.

Advertising signs on the road to Avila call it "The Best-Walled City in the World" *(la ciudad mejor amurallada del mundo)*. The publicity may be true, but there's more to Avila than the 1½ miles of fortifications, averaging 40 feet in height, with 88 towers and an

estimated 2,500 niches suitable for sentries or marksmen.

If you're visiting Madrid in summer, you'll appreciate the cooler mountain air of Avila—Spain's highest provincial capital, at more than 3,700 feet above sea level.

Before the "modern" Avila was built behind its crenellated wall, Celtiberians had settled in the area and are credited with having sculpted the crude stone statues of bulls and pigs around the city.

The **cathedral** of Avila, built between the 12th and 16th centuries, includes Romanesque, Gothic and Renaissance elements. It nudges the city wall; the apse, in fact, is a part of the wall itself. Fine stained-glass windows accentuate the grace of the interior. The choir stalls, carved to illustrate the lives of the saints, are attributed to the 16th-century Dutch master known as Cornelius de Holanda. The high retable was

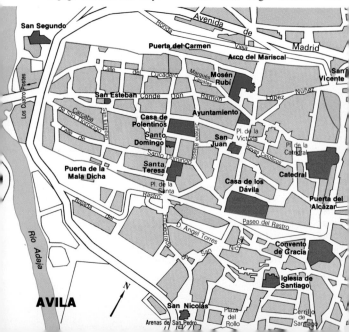

AVILA

begun by Pedro Berruguete, Spain's first great Renaissance artist, but he died in 1504 before it could be finished. The brightly coloured scenes from the life of Jesus were completed by later painters, Juan de Borgoña and Santa Cruz. In the ambulatory behind the altar is a brilliantly sculpted alabaster monument, the tomb of Bishop Alonso de Madrigal, whose dark complexion won him the nickname *El Tostado* (The Toasted One). The 16th-century sepulchre portrays the bishop in full regalia, accurate right down to the embroidery on his robes.

Attached to the cathedral, a museum of relics and art works includes sculptures, paintings and valuable illuminated manuscripts. The place of honour, in an inviolable glass case, belongs to a silver monstrance as tall as a man. Juan de Arfe* was the artist; 1571, the year he finished it, and the tiny bells all ring.

The **Basílica de San Vicente** (St. Vincent's Basilica), just outside the city walls, is considerably smaller than the cathedral, but hardly less inspiring. The main (west) portico features lifelike statues of the apostles—barefoot, long-haired, bearded men, seemingly caught off guard by a candid sculptor. Inside, an extraordinary tomb commemorates the historically hazy case of St. Vincent of Saragossa and his two sisters, martyred in the 4th century. Knights of old placed their hands on this 12th-century sepulchre when they took their oaths. Reliefs all the way around the tomb illustrate in abundant detail the suffering of the martyrs. All of this is topped by a bizarre oriental-looking canopy added in the 15th century.

Melancholy history surrounds the **Royal Monastery of St. Thomas** (south-east, down the hill), the construction of which was sponsored by Ferdinand and Isabella. Their only son, Prince Don Juan, died here at the age of 19. His tomb in the monastery was carved from alabaster by Domenico di Sandro Fancelli of Florence. In a small chapel close to it, poignantly, the prince's two tutors are buried. Elsewhere in the church, Pedro Berruguete painted the reredos, showing episodes from the life of St. Thomas. It's worth climbing the old stone stairs to the choir loft to see the wood-carvings, particularly on the seats reserved for

---

* Grandson of Enrique de Arfe (Heinrich from Harff, near Cologne), who created the monstrance of Toledo.

the Catholic Monarchs themselves. Their coat-of-arms (the yoke and arrows later adopted as the motif of the Falange) appears here and elsewhere in the monastery.

Another historical note: This royal monastery was the headquarters of the monarchs' confessor and adviser, the noted Friar Tomás de Torquemada. As the first Grand Inquisitor of Spain, he was the enthusiastic leader of the 15th-century witch-hunt.

St. Thomas's is a three-cloister complex. The first is a small cloister, leading to the Silence Cloister with its garden. Beyond this is the third cloister built as a summer version of the royal court. Here, in the regal rooms, the Dominicans now run the **museum** devoted to Oriental art. This is not as inappropriate as it may seem at first. The Dominicans have long done missionary work in the Orient, and this is their collection of art works discovered in the field. A friar in a white cassock will escort you around, pointing out exceptional items—a huge Vietnamese incense-burner, Chinese ivory carvings of superhuman intricacy, a great Japanese jar portraying a fierce samurai, ancient pictures from Nepal, a Chinese bell from the 5th century B.C.

Many visitors associate Avila with Santa Teresa de Jesús (St. Theresa of Jesus). A much-adored mystic, reformer and personality, Teresa de Cepeda y Ahumada was born in Avila in 1515. The Convent of St. Theresa was built on the site of her birthplace. She spent some 30 years in the **Convent of the Incarnation,** outside the city walls, as a novice and later as prioress. Amongst the other landmarks, the Convent of San José was founded by St. Theresa in 1562, the first of 17 Carmelite convents she eventually established. She was canonized in 1622 and proclaimed a doctor of the Church in 1970. In Avila, you can see relics and manuscripts and even the habit St. Theresa wore in a remarkable life of prayer, penance and poverty.

After you've seen Avila up close—the cobbled streets, the mansions, the storks' nests in the belfries—drive or take a bus across the River Adaja to the monument called **Los Cuatro Postes** (The Four Posts). The simple, columned structure, of forgotten historic and religious significance, is secondary to the location. From this rocky hill you look back on the entire panorama of medieval Avila. Only from this vantage point, or an airplane, can you encompass the whole city in one admiring gaze. Under the pale blue sky of Old Castile, the invulnerable walled city looks too fabulous to be true.

Left: black-bereted Avila street vendor deploys toy clowns at fiesta. Since Middle Ages, storybook walls have enclosed living city of Avila.

El Escorial
(49 km. west of Madrid)

More than a palace, the Escorial is an entire royal city—living quarters, church, monastery, mausoleum and museum—all under one roof. In a distinctly Spanish version of Italian Renaissance style, it sums up the physical and spiritual superlatives of the empire's Golden Age (see opening photo, pages 2–3).

King Philip II ordered the Escorial built in celebration of Spain's victory over French forces in 1557 at the Battle of St. Quentin, in France. The king himself died here in 1598, to be buried in a family tomb tunnelled beneath the high altar of the basilica. The royal pantheon contains the remains of almost all Spain's kings, queens, princes and princesses over a period of four centuries.

As sombre and vast as the royal palace may be, the overbearing effect is eased by the adjoining, non-royal town of San Lorenzo de El Escorial. At an altitude of 3,460 feet, it's a popular getaway spot for *Madrileños* escaping the worst

Tapestries based on Goya's designs adorn room in the Escorial palace.

of summer. For a town of only 7,000 inhabitants, therefore, it enjoys more than its share of hotels, restaurants and bars.

Sheer statistics don't do full justice to the extravagant scale of the royal palace complex, built in only 21 years. The longest wall is over 970 feet from slim corner tower to tower. The dome of the palace church rises 302 feet. By official count, the building contains 86 stairways, more than 1,200 doors and 2,600 windows. Contemporary Spaniards called it the Eighth Wonder of the World.

The first plan for the Escorial is credited to the architect Juan Bautista de Toledo, but he died only four years after construction began. His successor, Juan de Herrera, is considered the greatest Spanish architect of the age. He also built the Royal Palace of Aranjuez and reconstructed the Alcázar of Toledo.

Inside the **basilica,** shaped like a Greek cross, the mood is one of devout magnificence. The immense main retable is composed of red marble, green jasper and gilded bronze. Fifteen statues, lifesized or larger, were the work of Leone and Pompeo Leoni, a father-and-son team of sculptors from Milan. The Leonis are also responsible for the bronze group on either side of the high altar. These portray the family of Charles V (on the left side) and the family of Philip II, kneeling majestically in prayer.

The 124 finely carved seats in the choir include a slightly roomier one for Philip II. In all, the basilica, with its brightly painted vaulted ceiling, fulfils its mission of embodying the king's religious fervour. Of the dozens of art works collected here, none attracts more admiration than the life-sized marble crucifix by Benvenuto Cellini of Florence. It is said that the great Renaissance artist originally planned the statue to adorn his own grave.

Exactly below the high altar, at the bottom of a flight of marble stairs, the **Pantheon of the Kings** is a subterranean churchyard of history. In the central hall, identical marble sarcophagi are stacked four high. Gilded angels hold lamps illuminating the terse Latin inscriptions. Of all the Habsburg and Bourbon kings who ruled Spain, only two are missing (Philip V is buried at La Granja de San Ildefonso, Ferdinand VI in Madrid). Adjoining chambers are assigned to lesser royal personages, with a gloomy area devoted **71** entirely to the princes who died in childhood.

Above ground again, 40,000 rare books as well as manuscripts of immeasurable beauty and value are preserved in the **library** created by Philip II. The architect Herrera even took pains to design the bookcases, done in rare woods. The vaulted ceiling is a sight in itself—a painting symbolizing the arts and sciences, specifically Grammar, Rhetoric, Dialectic, Arithmetic, Music, Geometry and Astronomy. At opposite ends, Philosophy and Theology are extolled.

After seeing the church, mausoleum and library, visitors are shown through the **Palace of the Bourbons.** Here, one room is more lavish than the next. An outstanding element is the tapestries based on original designs by Goya and Rubens.

But the most striking wallcovering belongs to the **Hall of Battles.** Here, frescoes depict hundreds of soldiers, each detail carefully painted. The scene showing the Battle of Higueruela is based on the sketches by combat artists of 1431. Of course, the Spaniards won.

On the opposite side of the Courtyard of the Masks (named after the design of two fountains), the **apartments of Philip II** are modest in comforts, but rich in art works. The king died here among cherished paintings—a fantastic triptych by Hieronymus Bosch and works on religious themes by German, Flemish and Italian artists.

In addition to the fine paintings found elsewhere in the Escorial, the **New Museums** have been created to display the great works commissioned or collected by the Spanish monarchs. In the stately surroundings hang pictures by Bosch, Ribera, Tintoretto, Velázquez and Veronese. El Greco enthusiasts will find half a dozen of his canvases, including a unique portrait of Philip II at prayer in a sweeping celestial scene, as well as the classic *Martirio de San Mauricio* (Martyrdom of St. Maurice), full of sensitive detail. The New Museums amount to a worthy art gallery by any standards, a glorious afterthought to the historical and architectural significance of the Escorial.

Votive candles light faces of the devout in parish church near Avila.

Valle de los Caídos
(58 km. north-west of Madrid)

In a forested valley in the centre of Spain, Francisco Franco decreed that a memorial for the hundreds of thousands of victims, on both sides, of the Civil War be built on a site chosen personally by him. Thirty-five years later, in 1975, the Caudillo himself was buried beneath a simple stone slab in the monumental Church of the Valley of the Fallen. Officially, it is termed the "largest basilica ever built in the history of mankind", and this may be accurate. It was hewn out of the side of the mountain like a railway tunnel, yet claustrophobia is no great problem because the dimensions are so colossal and the decorations so unexpected.

The stone cross marking the basilica rises 492 feet from its base on top of a rocky outcrop. The cross is said to weigh 181,740 tons. Most other statistics are similarly impressive.

Farmer tills his land in idyllic countryside between Avila and Toledo.

From the parking area, where a souvenir shop sells Valley of the Fallen bottle openers and ashtrays, stairways lead to an esplanade with an area of 7½ acres. The arcaded façade of the church is big enough to fill one side of the esplanade. The style is reminiscent of Italian Fascist architecture. Inside the church, many statues and tapestries add to the subterranean pomp. There is plenty of room for decorations—the nave runs 860 feet into the mountain. Notable here are eight tapestries of the *Apocalypse of St. John* in brilliant colours. They were woven of gold, silver, silk and wool in Belgium in the mid-16th century and acquired by Spain's King Philip II.

A polychrome wood sculpture of *Christ Crucified* stands upon the high altar. The cross is said to come from a tree chosen and chopped down by Franco himself. Above this, the vast cupola is decorated by mosaics showing heaven-bound saints and martyrs of Spain.

Whatever your feelings are about the architectural, artistic, religious or political implications of the Valley of the Fallen, the superlatives add up to something unique and hard to forget.

Aranjuez

Pop. 30,000
(50 km. south of Madrid)

The deep-green water of the River Tagus, reflecting the noble buildings of Aranjuez, nourishes parks and formal gardens, as well as prize crops of asparagus and strawberries.

As you cross the bridge into Aranjuez on the road from Madrid, the roomy, geometric town plan becomes apparent. The balanced main square—actually a huge rectangle—is faced by arcaded buildings on two sides and the porticoed Church of St. Anthony at the south end.

But here the civic sights take second place to the royal parks and palaces. Ever since Ferdinand and Isabella, Spanish monarchs have been retreating to this oasis to escape Madrid's summer heat. Since the 18th century, they've enjoyed the luxury of a first-class country palace reminiscent of Versailles. In the mid-19th century, a railway line (later removed) ran right into the **Palacio Real** (Royal Palace). The iron horse was then considered so chic that it was a special delight for royal visitors to disembark directly at the bottom of the ceremonial staircase.

This is where the guided tours begin nowadays. They cover 22 rooms, enough to reveal a cross-section of royal taste in furniture, paintings, sculpture, tapestries, clocks, pianos, music-boxes and bric-a-brac. A few highlights:

Throne Room. All very ceremonious, except for the Louis XVI chairs beneath the royal canopy—surprisingly modest, really, for thrones.

Porcelain Room. Nobody could confuse this with any other room in any other palace. The decorations were created by the Buen Retiro porcelain factory of Madrid for King Charles III in 1760. The walls are covered with porcelain figures telling exotic stories: a Japanese samurai, Chinese mandarins, monkeys and birds. Seven mirrors, a weird porcelain chandelier, a circular couch and a fine marble floor complete the dazzling design.

Smoking Room. An Arabian Nights fantasy based on the Hall of the Two Sisters in the Alhambra at Granada. Red damask couches sprawl along the walls of this mid-19th-century reproduction.

Chinese Painting Salon. Hanging seven-deep along the walls, 200 ingenious rice-paper paintings were gifts from a Chinese emperor of the mid-19th century. The lantern-like chandelier, very original and oriental, comes from Japan.

A combined ticket covers all the sights in the palaces, gardens and museums. The **Museum of Court Dress,** downstairs in the Royal Palace, shows reproductions and, where possible, the actual costumes worn by Spain's kings and queens from the 16th to 20th centuries. One room is devoted to the costumes of the officials of the court—ambassadors, ministers, aides. A children's room decorated with the portraits of young princes contains their cradles, cribs and a rocking horse.

Less than 2 kilometres from the Royal Palace, the curiously named **Farmer's Cottage** *(La Casita del Labrador)* is set in the extensive Prince's Garden. Far from being a cottage, this is a condensed palace to which the kings retreated for parties and hunting weekends. Guided tours begin in the Billiard Room, filled by a behemoth billiard table illuminated by a formal chandelier.

Busts of ancient philosophers give the **Statue Gallery** its name, but the big attraction is what first seems to be a far-fetched fountain in the centre

Inspect Spanish regal fashions at museum in Aranjuez Royal Palace.

Salmer, Barcelona

of the room. It turns out instead to be a far-fetched clock, an 1850 folly, incorporating simulated water jets and a large music box.

This being an informal palace, the **ballroom** is scarcely large enough to accommodate 200 noble swingers. In their absence, a sturdy malachite desk and chair have been installed, a gift from the Russian Czar Alexander II to Queen Isabella II.

The **Platinum Room,** as sumptuous as it sounds, leads to the king's own toilet, wittily arranged as a plush throne.

Elsewhere in the Prince's Garden, in a modern building called the **Sailor's House** *(Casa de Marinos),* you can find out what became of the quaint "Tagus Squadron" of the royal fleet. The kings of Spain enjoyed being rowed down the river in gala launches. These flagships are preserved in the Sailor's House, along with related nautical mementoes. Here you can admire the last word in Rococo canoes, fancy feluccas and gilt gondolas.

Aside from the palaces and museums, Aranjuez is noted for its royal parks and gardens. The formal gardens are a wonder of flowers, clipped hedges, sculptures and fountains. The less disciplined forests of lindens, poplars or maples provide the kindest shade from the Spanish sun. **77**

Chinchón

A nice side-trip (20 km.) from Aranjuez, through gently moulded hill country, leads to Chinchón. Here is charming proof that you don't have to travel hundreds of miles from Madrid to immerse yourself in the Spain of cargo-carrying donkeys on cobbled lanes. The town square could be a stage set. The two- and three-storey white stucco houses with wooden arcades surround an irregular, but vaguely oval plaza. Watch the laundry being washed in the town fountain. In season, bullfights are held right in the square, changing its Wild-West image to Old Spain.

Chinchón is celebrated as the home of various aniseed liqueurs. It also grows a much-vaunted species of garlic, sold locally in strung bouquets.

Scattered around the countryside here you'll notice oversized earthen jars. These beehive-shaped vats, reminiscent of Roman amphoras, are made from a special type of clay quarried in this area. They're used for storing wine—or for decoration.

This Chinchón establishment sells ice-cream and more potent goods.

Three More Palaces

El Pardo, 15 kilometres northwest of Madrid, was the official residence of Generalísimo Franco for 35 years. It was built by Charles V in 1543 and reconstructed by Philip III after a fire in 1604. The main artistic attraction is a collection of tapestry amounting to hundreds of items; but to Spaniards, El Pardo may be more interesting for its memories of Franco's life—and death struggle.

La Granja de San Ildefonso, about 80 kilometres north of Madrid, is a huge palace set in classic formal gardens. Here, too, the tapestries—16th- to 18th-century masterpieces—are well worth seeing, collected by the Spanish royal family.

Riofrío, about 85 kilometres north of Madrid and 10 kilometres south of Segovia, has an 18th-century palace which is quite modest compared to the others. Part of it is now devoted to the **Museo de Caza** (Hunting Museum), with stuffed animals and ancient weapons. The palace is reached over the scenic road through the deer sanctuary. Drive carefully, and if you have any spare food along, the extrovert deer will eat out of the palm of your hand.

What to Do

Shopping

Madrid is Spain's superlative shopping centre, so leave some space in your luggage for gifts and souvenirs. What you buy will depend on your taste and budget, of course, but here's an alphabetical listing of items many visitors consider bargains or unique, or especially well made.

Alcohol. Bargains in brandy, sherry, wines and liqueurs bottled in Spain.

Antiques. Let the buyer beware, but Madrid's Rastro (flea market) attracts swarms of collectors. In nearby streets are more solid establishments dealing in old *objets d'art*.

Artificial pearls. From Majorca.

Bullfighter dolls, swords, hats—or posters, with your name imprinted as the star matador.

Capes. The old-fashioned Madrid *caballeros* sport a slightly sinister black version; women look glamorous in theirs.

Ceramics. Pots, bowls, tiles. Each Spanish region produces its own distinctive shapes, colours and designs, traditional or cheerfully modern. **79**

Damascene. Inlaid gold designs in steel—knives, scissors, thimbles, jewelry. Watch them being made in Toledo.

Embroidery. Good handkerchiefs, napkins, tablecloths, sheets, all embellished with deft needlework.

Fans. The collapsible kind, as fluttered by *señoritas* over the centuries.

Fashion. Spanish *haute couture* has gained a significant niche in international competition.

Glassware. Blue, green or amber bowls, glasses, pots and pitchers from Majorca.

Handicrafts. No end to the originality and skill shown in items on sale in Madrid, the best works from artisans.

Hats. An offbeat souvenir—a bullfighter or Andalusian hat, just for fun.

Ironwork. Heavy on the baggage scales, but lamps, lanterns and candlesticks are appealing.

Jewelry. From cheap hippy-made bracelets to the most elegant necklaces.

Knives. Penknives, daggers and swords from Toledo, where the Crusaders bought theirs.

Leather. Check the varieties of coats, hats, gloves, wallets, handbags.

Men's wear. Suits tailored

to individual order, if you have the time and the money.

Needlework. The traditional lace mantillas for special occasions; or hand-sewn lingerie.

Paintings. Dozens of galleries around town sell the works of contemporary Spanish artists.

Quaint Quixote statues and knicknacks are found in every souvenir shop.

Reproductions. Cheap but handsome copies of great Spanish paintings, on canvas, sold at the Prado and in shops.

Rugs. Inventively designed floor coverings, from tiny throw-rug to full-scale carpet. Some are hand-woven.

Shoes. No longer such a bargain, but styles are admired. Be careful of sizes, which tend to be narrow.

Suede. Coats and bags may strike your eye.

Traditional trinkets. Millions of tourists keep coming back for the same old novelties—miniature swords, plastic-lined wine-skins, castanets and, irrationally, imitation Mexican sombreros.

Underwater gear. Snorkels, masks, flippers are bargains.

Among shopping joys of Madrid: olives for all tastes (left) and a Rastro specialist in bric-a-brac.

Valencian porcelain. Distinctive figurines of traditional or fashionable modern subjects.

Wicker baskets. Something original for carrying your other souvenirs.

Woodcarving. Statues of knights or saints.

Young fashions. Spanish children may be the world's best dressed. On sale are charming clothes, but very expensive.

Zany zoological figurines. Sophisticated ceramic animals made in Madrid.

Where and When to Shop

For a quick survey of what Spaniards are buying, amble

through the major department stores, with branches around Madrid.

For a look at the range of handicrafts, covering paperweights to full suits of armour, visit a shop of Artespaña, the official chain of showplaces for Spanish artisans.

For elegance, shop along Calle de Serrano and neighbouring streets. For variety, try the shops in the Gran Vía.

Madrid's biggest department store chains, El Corte Inglés and Galerías Preciados, now operate from 10 a.m. to 8 p.m. (9 p.m. on Fridays and Saturdays) without a break. But most shops follow the traditional Spanish hours, about 9.30 a.m. to 1.30 p.m. and 4 or 5 to 8 p.m.

Tax Rebates for Visitors

The Spanish government levies a value added tax (called "IVA") on most items. Tourists from abroad will be refunded the IVA they pay on purchases over a stipulated amount. To obtain the rebate, you have to fill out a form, provided by the shop. You keep one copy; the three others must be presented at the customs on departure, together with the goods. The rebate will then be forwarded by the shop to your home address.

The Bullfight

The *fiesta brava,* the bullfight, is an enduring symbol of Spain—flamboyance and fate, and violence with grace. And Madrid is indisputably the world's bullfighting capital. No matter how much of a sensation a bullfighter may have achieved in the provinces, he's a nobody until he wins the cheers of the *Madrileños.*

You may not like what you see, you may swear never to return to it, or you may become an outright *aficionado.* Whatever your reaction, you'll have to admit there's nothing like it in the world: man against bull, skill against instinct. For the bull, the outcome is certain; for the matador, less so.

At the outset of the fight, the matador meets the bull, takes his measure and begins to tire him using the big red and yellow *capote.*

After these preliminaries, the first *tercio* (third) begins when the *picador,* a mounted spearman in Sancho Panza costume, lances the bull's shoulder muscles. Then, in the second *tercio,* the deft *banderilleros* stab long darts into the animal's shoulders.

In the third *tercio,* the

matador returns to run the bull through a long series of passes, using the small, dark-red *muleta* cape, eventually dominating the beast. Finally, as the bull awaits its death, the *torero* lunges for the kill.

Waiting his turn in the bullring, matador fidgets over his costume. Below: running the bull in Avila.

Depending upon the quality and bravery of his performance, the matador may be awarded an ear, two ears or, as top prize, two ears plus the tail.

You may be upset, fascinated or simply confused by an afternoon at the bullfights. Admittedly, the spectacle is not for everyone—not even for every Spaniard. But it is something that remains very much a part of Spanish life.

The larger and more celebrated of Madrid's bullrings, the Plaza Monumental at Las Ventas, seats 32,000 spectators. The other *plaza de toros,* Vista Alegre, is in Carabanchel.

Buying a ticket could be a problem. Your hotel desk clerk can usually help—but at a significant mark-up for the ticket agent and a tip for the clerk. Travel agencies run tours for the afternoon, which include transport, tickets and a commentary. However you go, and whether you sit in the *sol* (sun) or *sombra* (shade), invest a few pesetas in comfort:

Dancers at Madrid flamenco show sum up the passionate soul of Spain.

hire a cushion so you don't spend the afternoon sitting on bare concrete.

Normally, Sunday afternoon is *corrida* time. But during the San Isidro fiestas in May, Madrid outdoes itself with a bullfight programme every day for more than a fortnight. Tickets are hard to come by.

Flamenco

Spain's best-known entertainment, after the bullfight, is flamenco—throbbing guitars, stamping heels and songs that gush from the soul. Many of the songs resemble the wailing of Arab music—which may be a clue to flamenco's origins, though not all "flamencologists" agree.

Madrid's flamenco nightclubs attract crowds of enthusiasts, including tourists who don't usually go to nightclubs or stay up after midnight. The anguished chants and compelling rhythms generate an electricity which crosses all frontiers of nationality or language.

There are two main groups of songs: one, bouncier and more cheerful, is known as the *cante chico* (a light tune). The second group of songs, called *cante jondo*, deals with love,

death, all the human drama, done in the slow, piercing style of the great flamenco singers.

Purists say the talent in a *tablao flamenco* in Madrid is rarely up to top Andalusian standards. But it's a memorable night out, an overwhelming experience for the eyes, ears and heart.

Swinging Madrid

Europe's most indefatigable night people, the "cats" of Madrid, can choose from a profusion of bars and clubs. There are nightclubs with dancing girls, "intellectual" cafés, dark *boîtes* staffed with professional drinking partners, deafening discothèques, imitation pubs and beer halls, and jazz and folk-music clubs.

85

Travel agencies run Madrid-by-Night tours, taking in a couple of the top floorshows. Normally, the all-inclusive price covers dinner and a quota of drinks.

Casino

The Gran Madrid casino has turned the tables now, and American and French roulette, blackjack, chemin de fer and other games can be played in the swish halls of the casino, well purveyed with all the requisite bars, restaurants, etc. It's situated in the N-VI highway to La Coruña, half-an-hour's drive out of Madrid, and is open from 5 p.m. to 4 a.m. daily.

Cultural Activities

Concerts, Opera

Two resident symphony orchestras—the National Orchestra and the Spanish Radio and Television Symphony Orchestra—maintain a regular schedule of concerts for serious music fans in Madrid. Regular seasons of ballet and opera are also held.

Zarzuela

This uniquely Spanish form of operetta is much appreciated in Madrid, though its popularity has declined since the 1890's. The *zarzuela* comes in light-headed and in serious varieties. Even if you don't understand the language, it will entertain and enlighten.

Films

Almost all the films shown commercially in Spain have

Fiesta in windmill country of La Mancha brings out local folk dancers.

been dubbed into Spanish.

A certain number of cinemas in Madrid show foreign films in the original version, with Spanish subtitles. Normally, only avant-garde or controversial films are thus presented.

Theatre

Spain's dramatic tradition is long and glorious. In dozens of Madrid theatres, classical and contemporary foreign and Spanish works are performed, usually twice a night.

Fiestas

A fiesta in any Spanish city or village, however insignificant, will reveal a spirit and pageantry to be found nowhere else. If you happen to be around for the major spectacles, so much the better. But check local publications, ask at the tourist office or your hotel desk clerk to be sure you don't miss some unpretentious regional festival.

Here's a sample of noteworthy events in Madrid and surrounding provinces.

February

Zamarramala, Segovia Province. Santa Agueda festivals, medieval costumes and even older customs.

March

Illescas, Toledo Province. Fairs and bullfights for Festival of the Miracle of the Virgin of Charity.

March/April

Holy Week. Every town and city has striking processions of the penitent and other religious manifestations. In cities with famous cathedrals, such as Toledo and Segovia, the spectacle is unforgettable. The colourful town of Cuenca, 165 kilometres south-east of Madrid, is noted for its splendid processions and a religious music week.

May

Madrid. Fiestas of St. Isidore the Husbandman, the capital's patron saint. Half a month of neighbourhood parties, contests, plays, concerts and daily bullfights.

June

Toledo. Corpus Christi in Toledo. The Primate of Spain leads a solemn religious procession through the medieval streets.

Camuñas, Toledo Province. An ancient religious play is presented in mime, with spectacular costumes.

Segovia. Festivities of San Juan and San Pedro. Dances, bullfights.

July

Avila. Summer festival with poetry, art, theatre, sports, bullfights and funfair, all outdoors.

September

Candeleda, Avila Province. Pilgrimage of Our Lady of Chilla, medieval religious ceremonies plus dancing and bullfights.

October

Avila. Santa Teresa Week. Neighbourhood fairs, concerts, bullfights.

Consuegra, Toledo Province. Saffron Rose Festival in heart of windmill
country of La Mancha.

Sports

Half a dozen **golf** clubs in the Madrid area operate all the year round. The greens are open to non-members on payment of a fee. Instruction is available. For advance planning, ask the Federación española de Golf, Capitán Haya 9, Madrid, for a detailed pamphlet, entitled "Golf in Spain".

Elsewhere in Madrid, a variety of sports facilities cater to many interests. You'll find **tennis** courts, **polo** grounds, **squash** courts, **swimming** pools, **bowling** alleys and **riding** stables.

Spectrum of outdoor sports: fun at Madrid pool and intensely serious putting on the green at plush club.

Hunting and Fishing

Big-game hunters make advance arrangements to stalk the rare *capra hispanica* (Spanish wild goat) in the Gredos National Preserve near Avila. Closer to Madrid, red partridge is a popular target. Water fowl are protected in a national preserve near Ciudad Real. Consult the Federación Española de Caza, Calle de la Princesa, 24.

In rivers near Madrid run trout, pike, black bass and royal carp. For further information, contact the Federación Española de Pesca, Calle Navas de Tolosa, 3.

Hunting and fishing permits are available from I.C.O.N.A., Calle de Jorge Juan, 39.

Skiing

From December to April, the Guadarrama Mountains north of Madrid become a major ski area. The scenery and facilities are first-rate, and all equipment may be hired. The most highly developed resort is Navacerrada, only 60 kilome-

Left: an excited crowd cheers football titans, Real Madrid, playing on their home field. Right: watching the rowing-boats drift by in Retiro Park.

tres from Madrid by car or bus. The only snag is that the slopes are simply packed with *Madrileños* every weekend and on holidays. Several other areas within easy range of the capital may be less congested. For further information, consult the Federación Española Deportes de Invierno, the Spanish Winter Sports Federation, Calle de Claudio Coello, 32.

Spectator Sports

Car racing. Championship trials at the Jarama circuit, on the Burgos road, 26 kilometres north of Madrid.

Dog racing. Daily at the Canódromo Madrileño, Vía Carpetana, 57, Carabanchel.

Football (soccer). The No. 1 sport in Spain. Real Madrid plays at Santiago Bernabéu Stadium, Paseo de la Castellana. Atlético de Madrid uses the Vicente Calderón Stadium, Paseo de los Melancólicos on the river in southwest Madrid.

Horse racing. Afternoons at the Hippodrome of La Zarzuela, on the La Coruña road, 7 kilometres from central Madrid.

Pelota. The incredibly fast Basque ball game, known in some circles as *jai alai*. Afternoons at Frontón Madrid, Calle del Doctor Cortezo, 10.

For Children

Casa de Campo. Swimming pool, sailing lake, funfair, ultra-modern zoo. For added excitement, take the cable car soaring above the city (*teleférico* station in Paseo del Pintor Rosales).

Retiro Park. Hire a rowing boat or a bicycle; sniff the flowers.

Wining and Dining

Plenty of hearty food made with fresh ingredients at reasonable prices: Such is the good news awaiting hungry tourists or international gourmets in Madrid.* Restaurants in this melting pot of Spain reproduce all the country's regional specialities. The capital has many delicacies of its own, as well. And if you're homesick for a pizza, a curry or whatever, the foreign restaurants cover more than a dozen nationalities.

Meal Times

Madrileños eat later than anybody. Though breakfast runs a fairly businesslike 8 to 10 a.m., lunch rarely begins before 2 p.m. and can go on to 4 or 4.30 p.m. Dinner might be attempted at 9 p.m., but 10 or 10.30 p.m. is the usual hour to start. The secret to survival: snack bars and cafés which keep everyone going between meals.

Where to Eat

All Spanish restaurants are officially graded by forks, not stars. One fork is the lowest grade, five forks, the top; however, ratings are awarded according to the facilities available, not the quality of the food. Many fork symbols on the door guarantee spotless tablecloths, uniformed waiters, lavish lavatories and high prices—but not necessarily better cooking.

Cafeterías in Spain are not self-service restaurants, but modern establishments serving fast meals, mostly at a counter.

Tascas are bars serving sumptuous snacks with wine or beer (see page 93).

Cafés serve coffee, drinks and snacks, and are almost always open.

Eccentricities

Spaniards customarily pack away filling, three-course meals. Don't feel obliged to keep up the same pace.

Regional cuisine varies greatly, but Spanish cooking is never overly spicy; a few Spanish dishes, on the contrary, may seem under-seasoned. Pepper is rarely served at the table. Garlic enters the picture frequently but subtly.

Menu prices are "all-inclusive". Your bill automatically includes all taxes and service

---

* For a comprehensive glossary of Spanish wining and dining, ask your bookshop for the Berlitz EUROPEAN MENU READER.

charges. But it's still customary to leave a tip. Ten per cent is considered generous.

All restaurants (as well as hotels) have an official complaint form *(hoja de reclamaciones)* available to dissatisfied clients. To be used only in outrageous cases.

Tascas and Tapas

A *tapa* is a bite-sized snack; a *tasca* is where you find it. *Tascas* are all over Madrid, and contribute to the excitement and temptation. One minute a *tasca* is empty, the next a crowd is fighting for space at the bar, the waiters are shouting to encourage business, and debris is piling up on the floor. It's all part of the essential atmosphere.

You don't have to know the Spanish names, for you can simply point to what you want. In fact, in a few cases, it might be better not to know what it is that looks and tastes so delicious. There are snails, deep-fried squid, mushrooms fried in garlic, baby eels, tripe, prawns and garlic, cold potato omelet, potato salad, meatballs.

In *tascas,* the food is more

Atmosphere and hospitality follow tradition in Old Madrid restaurant.

important than the drink, served in small glasses. Draught beer or house wine is appropriate. And don't be shy about tossing your olive stones, mussel shells and used napkins on the floor. If you don't, the counter-man will!

Castilian Specialities

Cocido Madrileño may be distinctive to Madrid, but nevertheless resembles the hotpot or stew found in other regions of Spain. The meal often starts with *sopa de cocido* (the broth resulting from boiling the ingredients for the next course), then the *cocido* itself: beef, ham, sausage, chickpeas, cabbage, turnip, onion, garlic, potatoes.

Sopa Castellana is a baked garlic soup, not as strong as it sounds. At the last moment, a raw egg is added; by the time it reaches the table, the egg is well poached.

Callos a la madrileña. By any other name, stewed tripe. But the spicy dark sauce makes all the difference. A great local favourite.

Besugo al horno. Sea-bream poached in a wine sauce.

Cochinillo asado. Tender Castilian sucking pig roasted to a golden crispness.

Cordero asado. Roast lamb, often a gargantuan helping.

From the Regions

Andalusia: *Gazpacho* (pronounced gath-PAT-cho) is the famous "liquid salad", so refreshing on a summer day. A chilled, highly flavoured soup to which chopped tomatoes, peppers, cucumbers, onions and croutons are added to taste.

Valencia: Renowned *paella* (pronounced pie-ALE-ya) is named after the black iron pan in which the saffron rice is cooked. In with the rice will be such ingredients as: squid, sausage, shrimp, rabbit, chicken, mussels, onion, peppers, peas, beans, tomatoes, garlic. Authentically, *paella* is served at lunchtime, cooked to order.

Asturias: *Fabada*, a variation on Madrid's *cocido*, but based largely upon white beans and sausage.

Navarra: *Trucha a la navarra,* grilled trout with a surprise slice of ham inside.

Galicia: *Caldo gallego,* a rich vegetable soup. Almost all Madrid restaurants, incidentally, serve a delicious soup of the day—vegetable, bean, lentil or chickpea.

Basque country: All manner of rich fish dishes come from this gourmet region of northern Spain. Try *bacalao al pil pil* (cod in hot garlic sauce), or *merluza a la vasca* (hake in a casserole with a thick sauce), or *angulas a la bilbaína* (eels in a hot olive-oil and garlic sauce, always eaten with a wooden fork).

Left: Sucking pig in show window of Segovia restaurant. Below: bar in Madrid offers tempting seafood.

Desserts

Like the seafood, which is rushed to Madrid from the Atlantic and Mediterranean every day, fresh fruit from all parts of the country turns up on restaurant tables: oranges, peaches, pears, strawberries, grapes and melons. Pastries overflowing with whipped cream are easy to find, hard to resist. A local speciality in Avila, an egg-yolk sweet called *yema de Avila,* is monumentally rich. Toledo is famous for a sweet, nutty relic of the Moors, spelled here *mazapán.*

Cheese is very expensive in Spain, no matter where it comes from. Look for *queso manchego,* from La Mancha, in its several varieties, from mild to sharp. Native goat cheeses, mostly anonymous, are cheaper.

P.S.: Breakfast

The most insignificant meal of the day in Spain, breakfast is just an eye-opener. Typically, it's *café con leche* (half coffee, half hot milk) and a pastry, grabbed on the run at the counter of a local bar. In deference to foreign tastes, most hotels also serve a full breakfast of juice, eggs, toast and coffee.

As for breakfast pastries, try *churros*. These fritters are

Churros, left, are to be dipped. Musicians, below, are to be tipped.

often made before your eyes by a contraption which shoots the batter into boiling oil. You absolutely must dunk *churros* in your coffee. (In late afternoon, or in the early hours after a very late night out, the Spaniards love a snack of *churros* with very thick, hot chocolate.)

Beverages

You needn't give a thought to "winemanship", or matching wits with the wine waiter to choose just the right vintage. When the average Spaniard sits down to a meal, he simply orders *vino,* and it means *red* wine to the average waiter. Often served chilled, this house wine can go with fish or meat, or anything. Relax and enjoy the unpretentiousness.

The nearest renowned vineyards to Madrid are Valdepeñas. If you're in a Galician restaurant, experiment with Ribeira wine—heavy red or white, from the area near Portugal. In Basque restaurants or bars, look for Txacoli, a slightly sparkling white.

The most famous of Spanish wines is sherry from Jerez de la Frontera, which is fortified with the addition of brandy. As an aperitif, try a *fino*. An *oloroso* goes well after dinner.

Sangría, a summertime refresher, is a winecup or a punch made with red wine, fruit juice, brandy and slices of fruit, diluted with soda and plenty of ice.

Spanish beer *(cerveza)* is good and cheap; usually served quite cold.

Spain is a bonanza for spirits and liqueur drinkers. Many foreign brands are bottled under licence in Spain and cost very little. By cruel contrast, imported Scotch and Bourbon are ultra-luxurious.

You may consider Spanish brandy too heavy or sweet compared with French cognac. But it's very cheap—often the same price as a soft drink.

Spanish *cava*—white sparkling wine—is mass-produced and cheap.

If you prefer non-alcoholic beverages with your meal or at a café, have no qualms about ordering a soft drink or mineral water, or fruit juice.

Finally, look for *horchata de chufa,* a chilled, sweet milky-white drink made from ground-nuts which taste similar to almonds. It's always drunk through a straw. Many bars stock it in small bottles, but the *aficionados* look for a real *horchatería* where it's home-made. A splendid Spanish thirst quencher. **97**

To Help You Order...

Could we have a table? ¿Nos puede dar una mesa?
Do you have a set menu? ¿Tiene un menú del día?
I'd like a/an/some... Quisiera...

beer	**una cerveza**	milk	**leche**
bread	**pan**	mineral water	**agua mineral**
coffee	**un café**	napkin	**una servilleta**
cutlery	**los cubiertos**	potatoes	**patatas**
dessert	**un postre**	rice	**arroz**
fish	**pescado**	salad	**una ensalada**
fruit	**fruta**	sandwich	**un bocadillo**
glass	**un vaso**	sugar	**azúcar**
ice-cream	**un helado**	tea	**un té**
meat	**carne**	(iced) water	**agua (fresca)**
menu	**la carta**	wine	**vino**

...and Read the Menu

aceitunas	olives	**jamón**	ham
albóndigas	meatballs	**judías**	beans
almejas	baby clams	**langosta**	spiny lobster
atún	tunny (tuna)	**langostino**	prawn
bacalao	codfish	**lomo**	loin
besugo	sea bream	**mariscos**	shellfish
boquerones	fresh anchovies	**mejillones**	mussels
calamares	squid	**melocotón**	peach
callos	tripe	**merluza**	hake
(a la madri-	(with *chorizo*	**ostras**	oysters
leña)	and tomatoes	**pastel**	cake
cangrejo	crab	**pimiento**	green pepper
caracoles	snails	**pollo**	chicken
cerdo	pork	**pulpitos**	baby octopus
champiñones	mushrooms	**queso**	cheese
chorizo	a spicy pork	**salchichón**	salami
	sausage	**salmonete**	red mullet
chuleta	chop	**salsa**	sauce
cocido	meat-and-vege-	**ternera**	veal
madrileño	table stew	**tortilla**	omelette
cordero	lamb	**trucha**	trout
entremeses	hors-d'oeuvre	**uvas**	grapes
gambas	shrimp	**verduras**	vegetables

BLUEPRINT for a Perfect Trip

How to Get There

If the choice of ways to go is bewildering, the complexity of fares and regulations can be downright stupefying. A reliable travel agent can suggest which plan is best for your timetable and budget.

BY AIR

Scheduled flights

Madrid's Barajas Airport (see also p. 103) is on intercontinental air routes and is linked by frequent services to cities in Europe, North America, the Middle East and Africa.

Average journey times: Johannesburg–Madrid 12 hours, London–Madrid 2 hours, Los Angeles–Madrid 14 hours, Montreal–Madrid 6 hours, New York–Madrid 7 hours.

Charter flights and package tours

From the U.K. and Ireland: Many companies operate all-in package tours, which include flight, hotel and meals; check carefully to make sure that you are not liable to any surcharges. British travel agents offer guarantees in case of bankruptcy or cancellation by hotels or airlines. Most recommend insurance, too, for tourists who are forced to cancel because of illness or accident.

It you prefer to arrange your own accommodation and do not mind having to restrict your holiday to either one or two weeks, you can take advantage of the many charter flights that are available.

From North America: Package tours including hotel, car or other land arrangements can be very good value. In addition to APEX and Excursion fares, there's the Advance Booking Charter (ABC), which must be bought at least 30 days in advance.

BY ROAD

The main access road from France to Madrid is at the western side of the Pyrenees. A motorway (expressway) runs from Biarritz (France) via Bilbao to Burgos, from where you take the E25 straight down to Madrid, 240 kilometres (150 miles) away.

Express **coach services** operate between London and Madrid as well as between other European cities and Madrid. You can also travel by coach as part of a package holiday.

BY RAIL

The *Madrid-Talgo* links Paris with Madrid in about 11 hours. For most other connections you'll have to change trains at the border near San Sebastián.

Visitors from abroad can buy the *RENFE* (*Red Nacional de los Ferrocarriles Española,* the Spanish National Railways) *Tourist Card* for a reasonable price, valid for unlimited rail travel within the country for periods of 8, 15 or 22 days (1st and 2nd classes available).

The *Rail Europ S* (senior) card, obtainable before departure only, entitles senior citizens to purchase train tickets for European destinations at reduced prices.

Any family of at least 3 people can buy a *Rail-Europ F* (family) card: the holder pays full price, the rest of the family obtain a 50% reduction in Spain and 14 other European countries; the whole family is also entitled to a 30% reduction on Sealink and Hoverspeed Channel crossings.

Anyone under 26 years of age can purchase an *Inter-Rail* card which allows one month's unlimited 2nd-class travel.

People living outside Europe and North Africa can purchase a *Eurailpass* for unlimited rail travel in 16 European countries including Spain. This pass must be obtained before leaving home.

When to Go

If you can avoid Madrid in July and August—as many *Madrileños* do—you're more likely to carry away happy memories, as the heat can be stifling. In winter months, chill and greyness are often alleviated by bright, mild spells.

It is in spring or autumn that you are likely to find spectacularly delightful weather in Madrid: perfect temperatures, low humidity and some of the clearest sunshine in Europe.

Temperatures		J	F	M	A	M	J	J	A	S	O	N	D
average daily	°F	47	52	59	65	70	80	87	85	77	65	55	48
max. (afternoon)	°C	9	11	15	18	21	27	31	30	25	19	13	9
average daily	°F	35	36	41	45	50	58	63	63	57	49	42	36
min. (sunrise)	°C	2	2	5	7	10	15	17	17	14	10	5	2
Average hours of sunshine per day		5	6	6	8	9	11	12	11	9	7	5	4

Planning Your Budget

To give you an idea of what to expect, here's a list of average prices in Spanish pesetas (ptas.). They can only be *approximate,* however, as inflation creeps relentlessly up. Prices quoted may be subject to a VAT/sales tax (IVA) of either 6 or 12%.

Airport. Transfer to city terminal by bus 175 ptas., by taxi approx. 1,000 ptas.

Baby-sitters. From 500 ptas. per hour.

Car hire. *Seat Ibiza* 2,100 ptas. per day, 21 ptas. per km., 25,000 ptas. per week with unlimited mileage. *Ford Escort 1.1* 2,600 ptas. per day, 25 ptas. per km., 40,000 ptas. per week with unlimited mileage. *Ford Sierra 2.0* 4,700 ptas. per day, 47 ptas. per km., 54,000 ptas. per week with unlimited mileage. Add 12% tax.

Cigarettes. Spanish brands 100–150 ptas. per packet of 20, imported brands 175 ptas. and up.

Entertainment. Cinema 400 ptas. and up, theatre 700 ptas. and up, discotheque 1,000 ptas. and up, bullfight 2,000 ptas. and up, flamenco nightclub show (entry and first drink) 2,000 ptas. and up.

Hairdressers. *Woman's* haircut, shampoo and set or blow-dry 2,000–4,000 ptas., permanent wave 3,000 ptas. and up. *Man's* haircut 800–2,000 ptas.

Hotels (double room with bath per night). ***** from 10,000 ptas., **** from 9,000 ptas., *** from 6,000 ptas., ** from 3,500 ptas., * from 2,000 ptas.

Museums. Up to 500 ptas.

Restaurants. Continental breakfast 400–500 ptas., *plato del día* from 500 ptas., lunch/dinner in good establishment 2,500 ptas. and up, bottle of wine 200 ptas. and up, beer 25–200 ptas., coffee 85–125 ptas., Spanish brandy 125–200 ptas., soft drinks 110 ptas. and up.

Shopping bag. Loaf of bread 60–120 ptas., 250 grams of butter 325 ptas., dozen eggs 180–220 ptas., 1 kilo of beefsteak 1,400 ptas. and up, 100 grams of instant coffee 350 ptas. and up, 1 litre of fruit juice 200 ptas. and up, bottle of wine 250 ptas. and up.

Youth hostels. Approx. 1,000 ptas. per night.

An A–Z Summary of Practical Information and Facts

> A star (★) following an entry indicates that relevant prices are to be found on page 102.
>
> Listed after most entries is the appropriate Spanish translation, usually in the singular, plus a number of phrases that may come in handy during your stay in Madrid.

AIRPORT★ *(aeropuerto)*. Barajas Airport, 14 kilometres east of Madrid, handles domestic and international flights. Arriving passengers will find porters to carry their luggage to taxi ranks or bus stops. Taxis are readily available. Air-conditioned airport buses leave every 15 minutes for the city terminal beneath Plaza de Colón. The trip takes 30 to 45 minutes.

The airport buildings are provided with the usual amenities—souvenir shops, snack bars, car-hire counters, currency-exchange offices and hotel-reservation desks. There is also a duty-free shop.

Porter!	**¡Mozo!**
Taxi!	**¡Taxi!**
Where's the bus for …?	**¿Dónde está el autobús para …?**

A

BABY-SITTERS★. This service can usually be arranged with your hotel. Rates may vary, depending upon the hotel.

Can you get me a baby-sitter for tonight?	**¿Puede conseguirme una niñera (or, "canguro") para esta noche?**

B

CAR HIRE★ *(coches de alquiler)*. See also DRIVING. International and local car-hire firms have offices all over Madrid; your hotel receptionist can make arrangements. The law requires that you have an International Driving Permit, but in practice your national licence will probably be sufficient. Most agencies set a minimum age for car hire at 21.

C

C

A deposit, as well as advance payment of the estimated hire charge, is generally required, although holders of major credit cards are normally exempt from this. VAT or sales tax (IVA) is added to the total. Third-party insurance is automatically included, but you have to request full collision coverage. The customer pays for the fuel. Ask about any available seasonal deals.

I'd like to rent a car.	**Quisiera alquilar un coche.**
for tomorrow	**para mañana**
for one day/a week	**por un día/una semana**
Please include full insurance coverage.	**Haga el favor de incluir el seguro a todo riesgo.**

CIGARETTES, CIGARS, TOBACCO* *(cigarrillos, puros, tabaco)*. Spanish cigarettes can be made of strong, black tobacco *(negro)* or light tobacco *(rubio)*. Canary Islands cigars are excellent and Cuban cigars are readily available. Pipe smokers find the local tobacco somewhat rough.

The rights of non-smokers today prevail over the right to smoke; legislation makes it illegal to smoke in many public places in Spain. Always observe the no-smoking sign, whether on public transport, in department stores or cinemas.

A packet of …/A box of matches, please.	**Un paquete de …/Una caja de cerillas, por favor.**
filter-tipped	**con filtro**
without filter	**sin filtro**

CLOTHING. First, the climate problem. In winter, Madrid can be uncomfortably cold, not only because of the temperature but also on account of the mountain winds which carry the chill to your bones. Pack warm clothes. The summer is so dependably scorching that you won't need a sweater until the evenings in late August or September.

Madrid's traditional formality of dress has relaxed under the influence of the younger generation. Still, resort wear would be inappropriate in this big, sophisticated city. Some restaurants require ties for men, and jackets are suggested for the opera. On visits to churches, be sure to wear modest clothing—no shorts, for instance—though women no longer have to wear headscarves.

Will I need a jacket and tie?	**¿Necesito chaqueta y corbata?**
Is it all right if I wear this?	**¿Voy bien así?**

COMMUNICATIONS. Post offices *(correos)* handle mail and telegrams, but not normally telephone calls.

Post office hours: most post offices are open from 9 a.m. to 2 p.m.

Madrid's cathedral-like main post office on Plaza de la Cibeles stays open from 9 a.m. to 1.30 p.m. and from 5 to 7 p.m., Monday to Friday; Saturday from 9 a.m. to 2 p.m.

The special **lista de correos** *(poste restante or general delivery)* window at the main post office is open from 9 a.m. to 8 p.m., Monday to Saturday, and from 10 p.m. to noon on Sundays and holidays.

For telegrams the main post office stays open round the clock and for stamp sales until midnight.

Mail: If you don't know in advance where you'll be staying, you can have your mail sent to you *lista de correos* at the main post office. Mail should be addressed as follows:

> Mr. John Smith
> Lista de correos
> Plaza de la Cibeles
> Madrid
> Spain

Don't forget to take your passport as identification when you go to pick up your mail and be prepared to pay a small fee for each letter received.

Postage stamps *(sello)* are also on sale at any tobacconist's *(tabacos)*. Mail boxes are yellow and red.

Telephone *(teléfono)*. You can make local and international calls from public telephone booths in the street, from most hotels (often with heavy surcharges) and from some post offices. Area codes for different countries are given in the telephone directory. You'll need a supply of small change. For international direct dialling, pick up the receiver, wait for the dial tone, then dial 07, wait for a second sound and dial the country code (U.K. 44, Canada/U.S.A. 1), city code and subscriber's number. Madrid's main telephone office is located at:

Calle de Fuencarral and Gran Vía.
Open from 9 a.m. to 10 p.m. Monday to Saturday; from 10 a.m. to 2 p.m. and 5 to 9 p.m. on Sundays.

To reverse the charges, ask for *cobro revertido*. For a personal (person-to-person) call, specify *persona a persona*.

C **Telegrams** *(telegrama).* Telegram and post office counter services work independent hours and usually overlap. You can also send telegrams by phone—dial 222 2000. If you are staying at a hotel, the receptionist can take telegrams. Telex service is also available in principal post offices.

Can you get me this number in …?	**¿Puede comunicarme con este número en …?**
Have you received any mail for …?	**¿Ha recibido correo para …?**
A stamp for this letter/postcard, please.	**Por favor, un sello para esta carta/tarjeta.**
express (special delivery)	**urgente**
airmail	**vía aérea**
registered	**certificado**
I want to send a telegram to …	**Quisiera mandar un telegrama a …**

COMPLAINTS. Tourism is Spain's leading industry and the government takes complaints from tourists very seriously.

Hotels and restaurants: The great majority of disputes are attributable to misunderstandings and linguistic difficulties and should not be exaggerated. As your host wants to keep both his reputation and his licence, you'll usually find him amenable to reason. In the event of a really serious and intractable problem, you may demand a complaint form *(hoja de reclamaciones),* which all hotels and restaurants are required by law to have available. The original of this triplicate document should be sent to the regional office of the Ministry of Tourism; one copy stays with the establishment against which the complaint is registered, while the final copy remains in your hands as a record. Merely asking for a complaint form resolves most matters.

In the rare event of major obstruction, when it is not possible to call in the police, write directly to the Secretaría de Estado de Turismo, Sección de Inspección y Reclamaciones:

Duque de Medinaceli, 2, Madrid.

Bad merchandise and car repairs: Consumer protection is in its infancy in Spain. If you think you've been taken advantage of, all you can do is appeal to the proprietor.

In the event of gross abuse, take your complaint to the local tourist office. They're often able to sort out this kind of problem.

CONVERTER CHARTS. For fluid and distance measures, see page 110. Spain uses the metric system.

Temperature

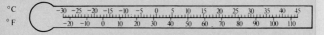

Length

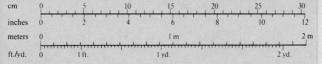

Weight

CRIME and THEFT. Spain's crime rate has caught up with the rest of the world. Wherever crowds collect in Madrid—at the Rastro or the bullfight, in buses and metro—be vigilant for handbag-snatchers and pickpockets. And remember never to leave luggage visible in a parked car.

I want to report a theft.	**Quiero denunciar un robo.**
My ticket/wallet/passport has been stolen.	**Me han robado mi billete/ cartera/pasaporte.**

CUSTOMS *(aduana)* **and ENTRY REGULATIONS.** Most visitors need only a valid passport to visit Spain, and even this requirement is waived for the British, who may enter on the simplified Visitor's Passport. Though residents of Europe and North America aren't subject to any health requirements, visitors from further afield should check with a travel agent before departure in case inoculation certificates are called for.

Currency restrictions. Tourists may bring an unlimited amount of Spanish or foreign currency into the country. Departing, though, you must declare any amount beyond the equivalent of 500,000 pesetas. Thus if you plan to carry large sums in and out again it's wise to declare your currency on arrival as well as on departure.

C   Here's what you can carry into Spain duty-free and, upon your return home, into your own country:

Into:	Cigarettes	Cigars	Tobacco	Spirits	Wine
Spain 1)	300 or	75 or	350 g.	1.5 l. and	5 l.
2)	200 or	50 or	250 g.	1 l. or	2 l.
Australia	200 or	250 g. or	250 g.	1 l. or	1 l.
Canada	200 and	50 and	900 g.	1.1 l. or	1.1 l.
Eire	200 or	50 or	250 g.	1 l. and	2 l.
N.Zealand	200 or	50 or	250 g.	1.1 l. and	4.5 l.
S.Africa	400 and	50 and	250 g.	1 l. and	2 l.
U.K.	200 or	50 or	250 g.	1 l. and	2 l.
U.S.A.	200 and	100 and	3)	1 l. or	1 l.

1) Visitors arriving from EEC countries.
2) Visitors arriving from other countries.
3) A reasonable quantity.

I've nothing to declare.   **No tengo nada que declarar.**
It's for my personal use.   **Es para mi uso personal.**

D   **DRIVING IN SPAIN.** To take your car into Spain, you should have:

- an International Driving Permit (not obligatory for citizens of most Western European countries—ask your automobile association— but recommended in case of difficulties with the police as it carries a Spanish translation) or a legalized and certified translation of your home licence

- car registration papers

- Green Card (an extension to your regular insurance policy, making it valid for foreign countries)

Also recommended: With your certificate of insurance, you should carry a bail bond. If you injure somebody in an accident in Spain, you can be imprisoned while the accident is being investigated. This bond will bail you out. Apply to your home automobile association or insurance company.

A nationality sticker must be prominently displayed on the back of your car. Seat belts are compulsory. Not using them outside towns makes you liable to a fine. You must have a red reflecting warning triangle when driving on motorways (expressways). Motorcycle riders and their passengers are required to wear crash helmets.

Driving conditions: Drive on the right. Pass on the left. Yield right of way to all traffic coming from the right. Spanish drivers tend to use their horn when passing other vehicles.

Main roads are adequate to very good and improving all the time. Secondary roads can be bumpy. The main danger of driving in Spain comes from impatience, especially on busy roads. A large percentage of accidents in Spain occur when passing, so take it easy. Wait until you have a long, unobstructed view.

Spanish truck and lorry drivers will often wave you on (by hand signal or by flashing their right directional signal) if it's clear ahead.

In villages, remember that the car only became a part of the Spanish way of life some 30 years ago; the villages aren't designed for them, and the older people are still not quite used to them. Drive with care.

Speed limits: 120 k.p.h. (75 m.p.h.) on motorways (expressways), 100 k.p.h. (62 m.p.h.) or 90 k.p.h. (56 m.p.h.) on other roads, 60 k.p.h. (36 m.p.h.) in towns and built-up areas.

Driving in Madrid: Nerve-wracking traffic jams are part of the way of life in the capital. To avoid the worst, try to drive in or through the city during the hours of the extended siesta afternoon break (usually between 2 and 5 p.m.). Madrid drivers are not noted for their courtesy. They are as impatient as drivers in Rome, but less skilled in avoiding accidents.

Parking: If driving in Madrid sometimes resembles a bad dream, parking is a positive nightmare as more and more central areas become "residents' parking zones" and non-residents have to buy parking tickets from the local tobacconists. The price—modest—depends on length of stay intended and different colours indicate different lengths of stay (maximum 1½ hours; any excess heavily fined). To make things worse, it's very often impossible to know that one is in such a zone (the signposts are not easy to understand) so the only way to be sure is to ask. And it's worth doing so: even tourists' cars don't always escape the *grua* that hauls away cars badly parked, and more than one tourist has returned to where his car was only to find no car, but in its place a parking fine with just a stone to keep it there. Underground parking facilities, ever more abundant, charge a fee.

D **Traffic police:** The armed Civil Guard *(Guardia Civil)* patrol the highways on powerful black motorcycles. Always in pairs, these tough-looking men are courteous and will stop to help anyone in trouble. They're severe on lawbreakers.

If fined, you will be required to pay on the spot. The most common offences include passing without flashing the directional-indicator lights, travelling too close to the car ahead and driving with a burnt-out head- or tail-light. (Spanish law requires you to carry a set of spare bulbs at all times.)

Accidents: In case of accident, dial the police emergency number, 092.

Fuel and oil: Fuel is theoretically available in super (97 octane), lead-free (95 octane), normal (92 octane) and diesel, but not every petrol station carries the full range. It's customary to give the attendant a coin or two as a tip.

Fluid measures

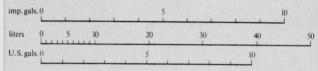

Distance

To convert kilometres to miles:

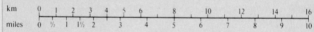

Breakdowns: Spare parts are most readily available for Spanish-built cars. For some other brands, spares may be difficult to find. Make sure your car is in top shape before you leave home.

If you have a breakdown on the highway, use one of the strategically positioned emergency telephones to call for help. Otherwise telephone the Guardia Civil.

Road signs: Most road signs are the standard pictographs used throughout Europe. However, you may encounter these written signs:

¡Alto!	Stop!
Aparcamiento	Parking
Autopista (de peaje)	(Toll) motorway (expressway)

Calzada deteriorada	Bad road
Calzada estrecha	Narrow road
Ceda el paso	Give way (Yield)
Cruce peligroso	Dangerous crossroads
Cuidado	Caution
Curva peligrosa	Dangerous bend
Despacio	Slow
Desviación	Diversion (Detour)
Escuela	School
Peligro	Danger
Prohibido adelantar	No overtaking (passing)
Prohibido aparcar	No parking
Puesto de socorro	First-aid post
Salida de camiones	Lorry (Truck) exit

(International) Driving Licence	**carné de conducir (internacional)**
car registration papers	**permiso de circulación**
Green Card	**carta verde**

Are we on the right road for …?	**¿Es ésta la carretera hacia …?**
Fill her up please, top grade.	**Llénelo, por favor, con super.**
Check the oil/tires/battery.	**Por favor, controle el aceite/ los neumáticos/la batería.**

I've had a breakdown.	**Mi coche se ha estropeado.**
There's been an accident.	**Ha habido un accidente.**

DRUGS. Until the 1980s, Spain had one of the strictest drug laws in Europe. Then possession of small quantities for personal use was legalized. Now the pendulum has swung back in the other direction: possession and sale of drugs is once again a criminal offense in Spain.

ELECTRIC CURRENT. Both 120- and 220-volt 50-cycle current may be encountered in Madrid, depending on the location and age of the building. Be sure to ask at your hotel desk before you plug in a razor or hair-dryer.

If you have trouble with an appliance, ask your hotel receptionist to recommend an *electricista*.

What's the voltage—120 or 220?	**¿Cuál es el voltaje—ciento veinte (120) o doscientos veinte (220)?**
an adaptor/a battery	**un adaptador/una pila**

E **EMBASSIES**

Australia:	Paseo de la Castellana, 143; tel. 279 85 04
Canada:	Núñez de Balboa, 35; tel. 431 43 00
Eire:	Claudio Coello, 73; tel. 276 35 00/8/9
South Africa:	Claudio Coello, 91; tel. 225 38 30
U.K.*:	Fernando el Santo, 16; tel. 419 02 08
U.S.A.:	Serrano, 75; tel. 273 36 00

Where's the ... embassy?   **¿Dónde está la embajada ...?**
American/Australian/British/   **americana/australiana/británica/**
Canadian/Irish/South African   **canadiense/irlandesa/sudafricana**

EMERGENCIES. If your hotel receptionist isn't handy to help, and you have a real crisis, dial the police emergency number, 091.

Here are a few other numbers for urgent matters:

Fire	080
Ambulance	274 14 29
Accidents (municipal police)	092

Depending on the nature of the emergency, refer to the separate entries in this section such as CONSULATES, MEDICAL CARE, POLICE, etc.

Though we hope you'll never need them, here are a few key words you might like to learn in advance:

Careful!	**¡Cuidado!**	Police!	**¡Policía!**
Fire!	**¡Fuego!**	Stop!	**¡Deténgase!**
Help!	**¡Socorro!**	Stop thief!	**¡Al ladrón!**

G **GUIDES and INTERPRETERS** *(guía; intérprete)*. Qualified guides and interpreters for individual tours or business negotiations may be hired through certain travel agencies or from Asociación Profesional de Informadores Turísticos:

Ferraz, 82; tel. 241 12 14.

We'd like an English-speaking   **Queremos una guía que hable**
guide.   **inglés.**
I need an English interpreter.   **Necesito un intérprete de inglés.**

* Also for citizens of Commonwealth countries not separately represented.

HAIRDRESSERS* *(peluquería)*/**BARBERS** *(barbería).* Some hotels have their own salons, and the standard is generally good. Prices vary widely according to the class of establishment, but rates are often displayed in the window.

Not too much off (here).	**No corte mucho (aquí).**
A little more off (here).	**Un poco más (aquí).**
haircut	**corte**
shampoo and set	**lavado y marcado**
blow-dry	**modelado**
permanent wave	**permanente**
a colour rinse/hair-dye	**champú colorante/tinte**
a colour chart	**un muestrario**

HOTELS and ACCOMMODATION* *(hotel; alojamiento).* Spanish hotel prices are no longer government-controlled. Accommodation in Madrid ranges from a simple but always clean room in a *pensión* (boarding house) to the luxurious surroundings of a five-star hotel. Hotel-reservation desks are found at Barajas Airport, at Chamartín and Atocha railway stations and in the Torre de Madrid on Plaza de España. Before the guest takes a room he fills out a form with hotel category, room number and price and signs it.

When you check into your hotel you might have to leave your passport at the desk. Don't worry, you'll get it back in the morning.

Other accommodation:

Hostal and **Hotel-Residencia:** Modest hotels without a restaurant, often family concerns.

Pensión: Boarding house, few amenities.

Fonda: Village inn, clean and unpretentious.

Parador: Government-run inn, usually in isolated or touristically underdeveloped areas.

Youth hostels *(albergue de juventud).* A youth hostel operates year-round in Casa de Campo Park. Normally, a stay is limited to three nights, and you must present a youth-hostel membership card. For addresses and other information, contact the Oficina Central de Albergues Juveniles:

Calle Ortega y Gasset, 71, Madrid.

113

H In central Madrid, cheap accommodation may be found at simple *pensiones* (boarding houses) and *casas de huéspedes* (guest houses).

a double/single room	**una habitación doble/sencilla**
with/without bath/shower	**con/sin baño/ducha**
What's the price per night?	**¿Cuál es el precio por noche?**

HOURS. See also under COMMUNICATIONS and MONEY MATTERS. One of the really great Spanish discoveries, aimed at keeping people out of the afternoon sun, is the siesta—just the ticket for overtaxed tourists as well as for locals. Try a nap after lunch.

But if you insist on fighting the system, you can still accomplish things between 2 and 5 p.m. The siesta hours are the best time to drive in or through Madrid (see DRIVING). Restaurants start serving lunch about 1 p.m. and dinner between 8 and 10 p.m.

Office hours: Generally from 9 a.m. to 2 p.m. and 4.30 to 7 p.m., Monday to Friday in winter; from 8.30 a.m. to 3 p.m. in summer.

Shopping hours: 9.30 a.m. to 1.30 p.m. and 4 or 5 to 8 p.m. Monday to Friday, 9.30 a.m. to 2 p.m. on Saturdays; department stores generally open from 10 a.m. to 8 p.m. without a break, Monday to Saturday.

Tourist Information Offices: 10 a.m. to 1 p.m. and 4 to 7 p.m., Monday to Friday, and 10 a.m. to 1 p.m. on Saturdays.

Museums: Most are closed on Mondays and public holidays.

L **LANGUAGE.** After Chinese and English, the most widely spoken language in the world is Spanish—at home from Madrid to Manila, from Avila to Argentina. The Castilian spoken in Madrid (seat of the all-powerful Royal Spanish Academy of the Language) is understood wherever you may travel in Spain.

French, English and German are widely understood in hotels and tourist-oriented establishments.

Good morning/Good day	**Buenos días**
Good afternoon/good evening	**Buenas tardes**
Good night	**Buenas noches**
Thank you	**Gracias**
You're welcome	**De nada**
Please	**Por favor**
Good-bye	**Adiós**

The Berlitz phrase book, SPANISH FOR TRAVELLERS, covers all situations you are likely to encounter in your travels in Spain. The Berlitz Spanish-English/English-Spanish pocket dictionary contains a 12,500-word glossary of each language, plus a menu-reader supplement.

Do you speak English?	**¿Habla usted inglés?**
I don't speak Spanish.	**No hablo español.**

LAUNDRY *(lavandería)* and **DRY-CLEANING** *(tintorería)*. Most hotels will handle laundry and dry-cleaning, but they'll usually charge more than a laundry or a dry-cleaners. In many areas of Madrid, you can find launderettes *(launderama)* which will wash, dry and fold a 5-kilo (11-pound) load of clothing.

Where's the nearest laundry/dry-cleaners?	**¿Dónde está la lavandería/ tintorería más cercana?**
I want these clothes cleaned/washed.	**Quiero que limpien/laven esta ropa.**
When will it be ready?	**¿Cuándo estará lista?**
I must have this for tomorrow morning.	**La necesito para mañana por la mañana.**

LOST PROPERTY. Check first at your hotel reception desk. Then report the loss to the police. In Madrid, all lost property should go to Plaza Legazpi, 7.

Lost children face few perils in Spain, where the people are particularly fond of youngsters. A lost child would normally be delivered to the nearest police station, which is where you should go if you lose a child—or find one.

I've lost my wallet/handbag/ passport.	**He perdido mi cartera/bolso/ pasaporte.**

MAPS. Road maps are on sale at most filling-stations and bookshops. The maps in this guide were prepared by Falk-Verlag, Hamburg, which also publishes a map of Madrid. The most detailed cartographic information is contained in the official atlas of Spain issued by the Ministry of Public Works.

A number of Madrid city maps are sold at news-stands. The municipal bus service issues a chart of all its routes. A city map with metro lines superimposed is posted outside every underground (subway) station, and a pocket-size map of the metro is available free on request at the ticket office in any metro station.

a street plan of …	**un plano de la ciudad de …**
a road map of this region	**un mapa de carreteras da esta comarca**

MEDICAL CARE. See also EMERGENCIES. To be completely relaxed, make certain your health-insurance policy covers any illness or accident while on holiday. If not, ask your insurance representative about travel insurance or have your travel agent arrange Spanish tourist insurance *(ASTES)* for you. *ASTES* covers doctor's fees and hospital treatment in the event of accident or illness.

For first-aid matters, paramedical personnel, called *practicantes,* can help. Hospitals, clinics and first-aid centres *(casa de socorro)* are concentrated in Madrid.

Pharmacies *(farmacia).* After hours, one shop in each area is always on duty for emergencies. Its address is posted daily in all other chemists' windows and published in all newspapers.

Where's the nearest (all-night) pharmacy?	**¿Dónde está la farmacia (de guardia) más cercana?**
I need a doctor/dentist.	**Necesito un médico/dentista.**
an ambulance/hospital	**una ambulancia/hospital**
I've a pain here.	**Me duele aquí.**

MEETING PEOPLE. Politeness and simple courtesies still matter in Spain. A handshake on greeting and leaving is normal. Always begin any conversation, whether with a friend, shop girl, taxi-driver, policeman or telephone operator with a *buenos días* (good morning) or *buenas tardes* (good afternoon). Always say *adiós* (goodbye) or, at night, *buenas noches* when leaving. *Por favor* (please) should begin all requests.

Finally, don't try to rush Spaniards. They have no appreciation for haste, and consider it bad form when anyone pushes them. Take your time. In Spain, there's plenty of it.

How do you do?	**Encantado de conocerle (Encantada** when a woman is speaking).
How are you?	**¿Cómo está usted?**
Very well, thank you.	**Muy bien, gracias.**

MONEY MATTERS

Currency. The monetary unit of Spain is the *peseta* (abbreviated *pta.*).
Coins: 1, 5, 10, 25, 50 and 100 pesetas.
Banknotes: 200, 500, 1,000, 2,000, 5,000 and 10,000 pesetas.

A 5-peseta coin is traditionally called a *duro*, so if someone should quote a price as 10 duros, he means 50 pesetas. For currency restrictions, see CUSTOMS AND ENTRY REGULATIONS.

Banking hours are from 9 a.m. to 2 p.m. Monday to Friday, till 1 p.m. on Saturdays.

Most Madrid banks have departments for changing foreign currency into pesetas. Curiously, the exchange rate for traveller's cheques is more favourable than for banknotes. Always take your passport with you; it's the only acceptable form of identification. Outside banking hours, you may use exchange offices *(cambio)* at Chamartín railway station, the airport or your own hotel. The exchange rate is a bit less favourable than in the banks.

Credit cards: All the internationally recognized cards are accepted by hotels, restaurants and businesses in Spain.

Eurocheques: You'll have no problem settling bills or paying for purchases with Eurocheques.

Traveller's cheques: Many hotels, travel agencies, shops and banks accept them—though in Madrid some branch banks refer clients to the head office. Remember to take your passport along for identification if you expect to cash a traveller's cheque.

Only cash small amounts at a time, and keep the balance of your cheques in the hotel safe if possible. At the very least, be sure to keep your receipt and a list of the serial numbers of the cheques in a separate place to facilitate a refund in case of loss or theft.

Prices: Although Spain has by no means escaped the scourge of inflation, Madrid remains quite competitive with the other tourist capitals of Europe.

Certain rates are listed on page 102 to give you an idea of what things cost.

Where's the nearest bank/currency exchange office?	**¿Dónde está el banco/la oficina de cambio más cercana?**
I want to change some pounds/dollars.	**Quiero cambiar libras/dólares.**

M

Do you accept traveller's cheques?	**¿Acepta usted cheques de viajero?**
Can I pay with this credit card?	**¿Puedo pagar con esta tarjeta de crédito?**
How much is that?	**¿Cuánto es?**

N **NEWSPAPERS and MAGAZINES** (*periódico; revista*). All major British and Continental dailies are sold in Madrid on their publication day. U.S. magazines and the Paris-based *International Herald Tribune* are also available.

The weekly *Guía del Ocio* lists information for Madrid visitors.

Have you any English-language newspapers?	**¿Tienen periódicos en inglés?**

P **PHOTOGRAPHY.** Most popular film brands and sizes are available, but they generally cost more than at home, so bring as much as you can with you.

The Spanish films Negra and Valca, in black-and-white, and Negra-color, are of good quality and cheaper than the internationally known brands.

In some churches and museums, photography is forbidden. If you go to a bullfight, be sure to sit on the shady side when taking pictures. You might need a filter to eliminate the red haze of the late afternoon sun.

Photo shops sell lead-coated plastic bags which protect films from X-rays at airport security checkpoints.

I'd like a film for this camera.	**Quisiera un carrete para esta máquina.**
a black-and-white film	**un carrete en blanco y negro**
a film for colour pictures	**un carrete en color**
a colour-slide film	**un carrete de diapositivas**
35-mm film	**un carrete de treinta y cinco**
super-8	**super ocho**
How long will it take to develop (and print) this film?	**¿Cuánto tardará en revelar (y sacar copias de) este carrete?**

POLICE (*policía*). There are three police forces in Spain: the *Policía Municipal,* who are attached to the local town hall and usually wear a blue uniform; the *Policía Nacional,* a national anti-crime unit recognized by their brown uniforms and berets; and the *Guardia Civil,* the national police force wearing patent-leather hats, patrolling highways as well as towns.

If you need police assistance, you can call on any one of the three. **P**
Spanish police are efficient, strict and particularly courteous to foreign
visitors.

Where's the nearest police
station?

**¿Dónde está la comisaría más
cercana?**

PUBLIC HOLIDAYS *(fiesta)*

January 1	*Año Nuevo*	New Year's Day
January 6	*Epifanía*	Epiphany
March 19	*San José*	St. Joseph's Day
May 1	*Día del Trabajo*	Labour Day
July 25	*Santiago Apóstol*	St. James's Day
August 15	*Asunción*	Assumption
October 12	*Día de la Hispanidad*	Discovery of America Day (Columbus Day)
November 1	*Todas los Santos*	All Saints' Day
December 6	*Día de la Constitución Española*	Constitution Day
December 25	*Navidad*	Christmas Day
Movable dates:	*Viernes Santo*	Good Friday
	Corpus Christi	Corpus Christi
	Inmaculada Concepción	Immaculate Conception (normally December 8)

In addition to these nation-wide holidays, Madrid celebrates May 2,
as well as its patron saint's day—San Isidro Labrador (St. Isidore the
Husbandman) on May 15—and *La Almudena* on November 9 as legal
holidays.

RADIO and TV *(radio; televisión)*. Most hotels have television **R**
lounges. All programmes are in Spanish, except for very occasional
showings of foreign films with subtitles.

Travellers with medium-wave receivers will be able to pick up the
BBC World Service after dark, from about 9.15 p.m. onwards. During
the daytime, both the BBC and the Voice of America can be heard on
short-wave radios.

R **RELIGIOUS SERVICES** *(servicio religioso)*. The national religion of Spain is Roman Catholic, but other denominations and faiths are represented. Services in English are held in the following churches:

Catholic: North American Catholic Church, Av. Alfonso XIII, 165

Protestant: British Embassy Church (Anglican), Núñez de Balboa, 43
   The Community Church (Protestant Inter-denominational), Padre Damián, 34
   Emmanuel Baptist Church, Hernández de Tejeda, 4

Jewish: The synagogue is at Balmes, 3

T **TIME DIFFERENCES.** Spanish time coincides with most of Western Europe—Greenwich Mean Time plus one hour. In spring, another hour is added for Daylight Saving Time (Summer Time).

Summer Time chart:

New York	London	**Madrid**	Jo'burg	Sydney	Auckland
6 a.m.	11 a.m.	**noon**	noon	8 p.m.	10 p.m.

What time is it?   **¿Qué hora es?**

TIPPING. Since a service charge is normally included in hotel and restaurant bills, tipping is not obligatory. However, it's appropriate to tip bellboys, filling-station attendants, bullfight ushers, etc., for their services. The chart below gives some suggestions as to what to leave.

Hotel porter, per bag	minimum 50 ptas.
Maid, for extra services	100–200 ptas.
Lavatory attendant	25–50 ptas.
Waiter	10% (optional)
Taxi driver	10%
Hairdresser/Barber	10%
Tourist guide	10%

Keep the change.   **Déjelo para usted.**

TOILETS. There are many expressions for toilets in Spanish: *aseos, servicios, W.C., water* and *retretes*. The first two terms are the most common.

In public conveniences, attendants expect a small tip. If you drop into a bar specifically to use the facilities, it is considered polite to buy a cup of coffee or a glass of wine as well.

Where are the toilets? **¿Dónde están los servicios?**

TOURIST INFORMATION OFFICES *(oficinas de turismo)*. Spanish National Tourist Offices are maintained in many countries throughout the world. These offices will supply you with a wide range of colourful and informative brochures and maps in English on the various towns and regions in Spain. They will also let you consult a copy of the master directory of hotels in Spain, listing all facilities and prices.

Canada: 60 Bloor St. West, Suite 201, Toronto, Ont. M4W 3B8; tel. (416) 961-3131.

United Kingdom: 57, St. James's St. London S.W.1; tel. (01) 499-0901.

U.S.A.: 845 N. Michigan Ave., Chicago, IL 60611; tel. (312) 944-0215.
4800 The Galleria, 5085 Westheimer Rd., Houston, TX 77056; tel. (713) 840-7411.
665 5th Ave., New York, N.Y. 10022; tel. (212) 759-8822.

Tourist information offices in Madrid:
Torre de Madrid (Plaza de España); tel. 241 23 25
Calle Duque de Medinaceli, 2; tel. 429 49 51
Chamartín railway station
Barajas Airport; tel. 205 83 56

On-the-spot advice is available from multilingual experts who patrol the streets of tourist zones. Look for the blue-and-yellow uniform with the **i** symbol on the lapel.

TRANSPORT

Buses *(autobús)*. The municipal transportation system, EMT, operates bus routes criss-crossing Madrid. On blue buses, you generally enter through the rear door and buy a ticket from a conductor seated behind a little desk. On red ones, you enter by the front door and pay the driver. Municipal buses operate from about 5.30 a.m. to 1.30 a.m. **121**

T A bargain ticket *(Bono Bus),* valid for ten rides on the red buses, is available at EMT booths—or, at a fractionally higher price, on buses with conductors.

Microbuses *(microbús).* These small, yellow buses are air-conditioned and more manœuvrable than conventional buses, hence faster and slightly more expensive.

Metro: Madrid's underground (subway) system combines speed with economy. The catch is that the metro can be oven-hot in summer. For the metro, too, there is a cheaper ten-ride ticket *(Billete de diez viajes).* Ask for a metro map at any station.

Taxi *(taxi).* Madrid's 12,000 taxis are easily recognized by the letters *SP* (for *servicio público*) on front and rear bumpers, the symbol of Madrid's bear on the rear doors and the livery—the taxicabs are painted either black or white with a red stripe. If a taxi is free, a green light on the right front corner of the roof is turned on and a *libre* ("free") sign is displayed.

The meter shows an initial charge at the drop of the flag, with fares varying according to distance and time elapsed. The figure displayed at the end of your trip may not be the full price. Legitimate added charges are compounded for night and holiday travel, pickups, etc.

Non-metered tourist cars, which often solicit business at major hotels and nightclubs, charge premium rates.

Trains *(tren).* Madrid's three principal railway stations are Chamartín (just off the Paseo de la Castellana). Norte (facing the Campo del Moro) and Atocha (south of the Prado). In general, rail service to nearby towns of interest is less convenient than parallel bus services. But the luxurious international *Talgo* and the long-distance *Ter* trains are highly regarded. Seat reservations are required for most Spanish trains.

EuroCity (EC)	International express, first and second classes
Talgo, Intercity, Electrotren, Ter, Tren Estrella	Luxury diesel, first and second classes; supplementary charge over regular fare

Expreso, Rápido	Long-distance expresses, stopping at main stations only; supplementary charge, usually second class only
Omnibus, Tranvía, Automotor	Local trains, with frequent stops, usually second class only
Auto Expreso	Car train
Coche cama	Sleeping-car with 1-, 2- or 3-bedded compartments, washing facilities
Coche comedor	Dining-car
Litera	Sleeping-berth car *(couchette)* with blankets, sheets and pillows
Furgón de equipajes	Luggage van (baggage car); only registered luggage permitted

When's the next bus to …?	**¿Cuándo sale el próximo autobús para …?**
Will you tell me when to get off?	**¿Podría indicarme cuándo tengo que bajar?**
Where can I get a taxi?	**¿Dónde puedo coger un taxi?**
What's the fare to …?	**¿Cuánto es la tarifa a …?**
Which is the best train to …?	**Cuál es el mejor tren para …?**
I want a ticket to …	**Quiero un billete para …**
single (one-way)	**ida**
return (round-trip)	**ida y vuelta**
first/second class	**primera/segunda clase**
I'd like to make seat reservations.	**Quiero reservar asientos.**

WATER *(agua)*. Madrid's mountain spring water is less delicious nowadays because of chlorination. You can drink it from the tap with confidence. Spaniards often prefer bottled mineral water, which is tasty and healthful.

DAYS OF THE WEEK

Sunday	**domingo**	Wednesday	**miércoles**
Monday	**lunes**	Thursday	**jueves**
Tuesday	**martes**	Friday	**viernes**
		Saturday	**sábado**

MONTHS

January	**enero**	July	**julio**
February	**febrero**	August	**agosto**
March	**marzo**	September	**septiembre**
April	**abril**	October	**octubre**
May	**mayo**	November	**noviembre**
June	**junio**	December	**diciembre**

NUMBERS

0	**cero**	18	**dieciocho**
1	**uno**	19	**diecinueve**
2	**dos**	20	**veinte**
3	**tres**	21	**veintiuno**
4	**cuatro**	22	**veintidós**
5	**cinco**	30	**treinta**
6	**seis**	31	**treinta y uno**
7	**siete**	32	**treinta y dos**
8	**ocho**	40	**cuarenta**
9	**nueve**	50	**cincuenta**
10	**diez**	60	**sesenta**
11	**once**	70	**setenta**
12	**doce**	80	**ochenta**
13	**trece**	90	**noventa**
14	**catorce**	100	**cien**
15	**quince**	101	**ciento uno**
16	**dieciséis**	500	**quinientos**
17	**diecisiete**	1,000	**mil**

SOME USEFUL EXPRESSIONS

yes/no	**sí/no**
please/thank you	**por favor/gracias**
excuse me/you're welcome	**perdone/de nada**
where/when/how	**dónde/cuándo/cómo**
how long/how far	**cuánto tiempo/a qué distancia**
yesterday/today/tomorrow	**ayer/hoy/mañana**
day/week/month/year	**día/semana/mes/año**
left/right	**izquierda/derecha**
up/down	**arriba/abajo**
good/bad	**bueno/malo**
big/small	**grande/pequeño**
cheap/expensive	**barato/caro**
hot/cold	**caliente/frío**
old/new	**viejo/nuevo**
open/closed	**abierto/cerrado**
here/there	**aquí/allí**
free (vacant)/occupied	**libre/ocupado**
early/late	**temprano/tarde**
easy/difficult	**fácil/difícil**
Does anyone here speak English?	**¿Hay alguien aquí que hable inglés?**
What does this mean?	**¿Qué quiere decir esto?**
I don't understand.	**No comprendo.**
Please write it down.	**Escríbamelo, por favor.**
Is there an admission charge?	**¿Se debe pagar la entrada?**
Waiter!/Waitress!	**¡Camarero!/¡Camarera!**
I'd like ...	**Quisiera ...**
How much is that?	**¿Cuánto es?**
Have you something less expensive?	**¿Tiene algo más barato?**
Just a minute.	**Un momento.**
Help me please.	**Ayúdeme, por favor.**
Get a doctor quickly.	**¡Llamen a un médico, rápidamente!**

Index

An asterisk (*) next to a page number indicates a map reference. For index to practical information, see inside front cover.

108/908 RP

Selection of Madrid Hotels and Restaurants

Where do you start? Choosing a hotel or restaurant in a place you're not familiar with can be daunting. To help you find your way amid the bewildering variety, we have made a selection from the *Red Guide to Portugal and Spain 1988* published by Michelin, the recognized authority on gastronomy and accommodation throughout Europe.

Our own Berlitz criteria have been (a) price and (b) location. In the hotel section, for a double room with bath but without breakfast, Higher-priced means above ptas. 10,000, Medium-priced ptas. 6,000–10,000, Lower-priced below ptas. 6,000. As to restaurants, for a meal consisting of a starter, a main course and a dessert, Higher-priced means above ptas. 4,000, Medium-priced ptas. 3,000–4,000, Lower-priced below ptas. 3,000. Special features (where applicable), and regular closing days are also given. For hotels and restaurants, checking first to make certain that they are open and advance reservations are both advisable. In Spain, hotel and restaurant prices include a service charge, but a value-added tax (IVA) of 6–12% will also automatically be added to the bill.

For a wider choice of hotels and restaurants, we strongly recommend you obtain the authoritative Michelin *Red Guide to Portugal and Spain,* which gives a comprehensive and reliable picture of the situation throughout the country.

HOTELS

HIGHER-PRICED
(above ptas. 10,000)

Alcalá
Alcalá 66
28009 Madrid
Tel. 435 10 60; tlx. 48094
153 rooms
Basque restaurant.

Emperador
Gran Vía 53
28013 Madrid
Tel. 247 28 00; tlx. 46261
232 rooms
Outdoor swimming pool. No restaurant.

Eurobuilding
Padre Damián 23
28036 Madrid
Tel. 457 78 00; tlx. 22548
540 rooms
Garden and terrace with outdoor swimming pool.

G. H. Velázquez
Velázquez 62
28001 Madrid
Tel. 275 28 00; tlx. 22779
145 rooms

Holiday Inn
av. General Perón
28020 Madrid
Tel. 456 70 14; tlx. 44709
310 rooms
Dinner accompanied by piano music. Outdoor swimming pool.

Meliá Castilla
Capitán Haya 43
28020 Madrid
Tel. 571 22 11; tlx. 23142
1,000 rooms
Outdoor swimming pool.

Meliá Madrid
Princesa 27
28008 Madrid
Tel. 241 82 00; tlx. 22537
265 rooms
Outdoor dining.

Miguel Angel
Miguel Angel 31
28010 Madrid
Tel. 442 00 22; tlx. 44235
300 rooms
Indoor swimming pool.

Mindanao
paseo San Francisco de Sales 15
28003 Madrid
Tel. 449 55 00 ; tlx. 22631
289 rooms
Outdoor and indoor swimming pools.

Novotel Madrid
Albacete 1
28027 Madrid
Tel. 405 46 00; tlx. 41862
240 rooms
Outdoor dining. Outdoor swimming pool.

Palace
pl. de las Cortes 7
28014 Madrid
Tel. 429 75 51; tlx. 22272
508 rooms

Pintor
Goya 79
28001 Madrid
Tel. 435 75 45; tlx. 23281
176 rooms

Plaza
pl. de España
28013 Madrid
Tel. 247 12 00; tlx. 27383
306 rooms
*View. Outdoor swimming pool
(summer only). No restaurant,
but snacks available.*

Princesa Plaza
Serrano Jover 3
28015 Madrid
Tel. 242 21 00; tlx. 44377
406 rooms

Ritz
pl. de la Lealtad 5
28014 Madrid
Tel. 521 28 57; tlx. 43986
156 rooms
Pleasant hotel. Outdoor dining.

Sanvy
Goya 3
28001 Madrid
Tel. 276 08 00; tlx. 44994
141 rooms
*Outdoor swimming pool. Belagua
restaurant.*

Suecia
Marqués de Casa Riera 4
28014 Madrid
Tel. 231 69 00; tlx. 22313
67 rooms
Bellman restaurant.

Villa Magna
paseo de la Castellana 22
28046 Madrid
Tel. 261 49 00; tlx. 22914
198 rooms
Pleasant hotel.

Wellington
Velázquez 8
28001 Madrid
Tel. 275 44 00; tlx. 22700
258 rooms
*Outdoor swimming pool. El Fogón
restaurant.*

OUTSKIRTS OF MADRID

Monte Real
Arroyofresno 17
28035 Madrid
Tel. 216 21 40; tlx. 22089
79 rooms
*Quiet hotel. Elegant decor.
Outdoor dining. Pretty garden.
Outdoor swimming pool.*

MEDIUM-PRICED
(ptas. 6,000–10,000)

Abeba
Alcántara 63
28006 Madrid
Tel. 401 16 50
100 rooms
No restaurant.

Agumar
paseo Reina Cristina 9
28014 Madrid
Tel. 552 69 00; tlx. 22814
252 rooms
No restaurant, but snacks available

Apartotel El Jardín
carret. N1
28034 Madrid
Tel. 202 83 36
41 rooms
Outdoor swimming pool. Garden. Hotel tennis courts. No restaurant.

Aramo
paseo Santa María de la Cabeza 73
28045 Madrid
Tel. 473 91 11; tlx. 45885
105 rooms
No restaurant, but snacks available.

Aristos
av. Pio XII-34
28016 Madrid
Tel. 457 04 50
24 rooms
Outdoor dining. El Chaflán restaurant.

Arosa
Salud 21
28013 Madrid
Tel. 232 16 00; tlx. 43618
126 rooms
No restaurant, but snacks available.

Bretón
Bretón de los Herreros 29
28003 Madrid
Tel. 442 83 00
56 rooms
No restaurant.

Capitol
Gran Vía 41
28013 Madrid
Tel. 521 83 91; tlx. 41499
142 rooms
No restaurant.

Carlos V
Maestro Vitoria 5
28013 Madrid
Tel. 231 41 00; tlx. 48547
67 rooms
No restaurant.

Carlton
paseo de las Delicias 26
28045 Madrid
Tel. 239 71 00; tlx. 44571
133 rooms

Chamartín
estación de Chamartín
28036 Madrid
Tel. 733 90 11; tlx. 49201
378 rooms
No restaurant.

Conde Duque
pl. Conde Valle de Suchil 5
28015 Madrid
Tel. 447 70 00; tlx. 22058
138 rooms
No restaurant, but snacks available.

Convención
O'Donnell 53
28009 Madrid
Tel. 274 68 00; tlx. 23944
790 rooms
*No restaurant, but snacks
available.*

El Coloso
Leganitos 13
28013 Madrid
Tel. 248 76 00; tlx. 47017
84 rooms

El Gran Atlanta
Comandanta Zorita 34
28020 Madrid
Tel. 253 59 00; tlx. 45210
180 rooms
No restaurant.

El Prado
Prado 11
28014 Madrid
Tel. 429 35 68
45 rooms
No restaurant.

Emperatriz
López de Hoyos 4
28006 Madrid
Tel. 413 65 11; tlx. 43640
170 rooms
*No restaurant, but snacks
available.*

G. H. Colón
Pez Volador 11
28007 Madrid
Tel. 273 59 00; tlx. 22984
390 rooms
Outdoor swimming pool. Garden.

Las Alondras
José Abascal 8
28003 Madrid
Tel. 447 40 00; tlx. 49454
72 rooms
*No restaurant, but snacks
available.*

Liabeny
Salud 3
28013 Madrid
Tel. 232 53 06; tlx. 49024
158 rooms

Mayorazgo
Flor Baja 3
28013 Madrid
Tel. 247 26 00; tlx. 45647
200 rooms

Príncipe Pío
cuesta de San Vicente 16
28008 Madrid
Tel. 247 08 00; tlx. 42183
157 rooms

Puerta de Toledo
glorieta Puerta de Toledo 4
28005 Madrid
Tel. 474 71 00; tlx. 22291
152 rooms
Puerta de Toledo restaurant.

Washington
Gran Vía 72
28013 Madrid
Tel. 266 71 00; tlx. 48773
120 rooms
No restaurant.

Zurbano
Zurbano 79
28003 Madrid
Tel. 441 55 00; tlx. 27578
261 rooms

LOWER-PRICED
(below ptas. 6,000)

Alexandra
San Bernardo 29
28015 Madrid
Tel. 242 04 00
69 rooms
No restaurant.

Amberes
Gran Vía 68 – 7° piso
28013 Madrid
Tel. 247 61 00
44 rooms
No restaurant.

Anaco
Tres Cruces 3
28013 Madrid
Tel. 522 46 04
37 rooms
No restaurant.

Atlántico
Gran Vía 38 – 3° piso
28013 Madrid
Tel. 522 64 80; tlx. 43142
62 rooms
No restaurant.

California
Gran Vía 38 – 1° piso
28013 Madrid
Tel. 522 47 03
26 rooms
No restaurant.

Casón del Tormes
Río 7
28013 Madrid
Tel. 241 97 46
61 rooms
No restaurant.

Claridge
pl. del Conde de Casal 6
28007 Madrid
Tel. 551 94 00; tlx. 45585
150 rooms
No restaurant, but snacks available.

Cortezo
Dr Cortezo 3
28012 Madrid
Tel. 239 38 00; tlx. 48704
90 rooms
No restaurant, but snacks available.

Don Diego
Velázquez 45 – 5° piso
28001 Madrid
Tel. 435 07 60
58 rooms
No restaurant.

Francisco I
Arenal 15
28013 Madrid
Tel. 248 02 04; tlx. 43448
57 rooms

Galicia
Valverde 1 – 4° piso
28004 Madrid
Tel. 522 10 13
40 rooms
No restaurant.

Hostal Auto
paseo de la Chopera 69
28045 Madrid
Tel. 239 66 00
106 rooms
Mesón Auto restaurant.

Inglés
Echegaray 10
28014 Madrid
Tel. 429 65 51
58 rooms
No restaurant.

Italia
Gonzálo Jiménez de Quesada 2 –
2° piso
28004 Madrid
Tel. 522 47 90
59 rooms

Lisboa
Ventura de la Vega 17
28014 Madrid
Tel. 429 46 76
23 rooms
*No restaurant. Breakfast not
provided.*

Lope de Vega
Gran Vía 59 – 9° piso
28013 Madrid
Tel. 247 70 00
47 rooms
View. No restaurant.

Madrid
Carretas 10
28012 Madrid
Tel. 521 65 20; tlx. 43142
72 rooms
No restaurant.

Mercator
Atocha 123
28012 Madrid
Tel. 429 05 00; tlx. 46129
90 rooms
*No restaurant, but snacks
available.*

Moderno
Arenal 2
28013 Madrid
Tel. 231 09 00
98 rooms
No restaurant.

Paris
Alcalá 2
28014 Madrid
Tel. 521 64 96; tlx. 43448
114 rooms

Persal
pl. del Angel 12
28012 Madrid
Tel. 230 31 08
100 rooms
No restaurant.

Praga
Antonio López 65
28019 Madrid
Tel. 469 06 00; tlx. 45248
428 rooms
*No restaurant, but snacks
available.*

Santander
Echegaray 1
28014 Madrid
Tel. 429 95 51
38 rooms
No restaurant.

Tirol
Marqués de Urquijo 4
28008 Madrid
Tel. 248 19 00
93 rooms
*No restaurant, but snacks
available.*

RESTAURANTS

HIGHER-PRICED
(above ptas. 4,000)

Bajamar
Gran Via 78
28013 Madrid
Tel. 248 59 03; tlx. 22818
Fish and shellfish.

Bidasoa
Claudio Coello 24
28001 Madrid
Tel. 431 20 81; tlx. 42948
Closed Sunday.

Cabo Mayor
Juan Hurtado de Mendoza 11
28036 Madrid
Tel. 250 87 76; tlx. 49784
Notably good cuisine. Original decor.

Café de Chinitas
Torija 7
28013 Madrid
Tel. 248 51 35
Dinner only. Flamenco. Supplement payable for floorshow. Closed Sunday and Christmas Eve.

Café de Oriente
pl. de Oriente 2
28013 Madrid
Tel. 241 39 74
Notably good, Basque-French cuisine. Elegant decor. Closed Saturday lunchtime, Sunday and August.

Club 31
Alcalá 58
28014 Madrid
Tel. 231 00 92
Closed August.

Don Victor
Emilio Vargas 18
28043 Madrid
Tel. 415 47 47
Outdoor dining. Closed Saturday lunchtime, Sunday and August.

El Amparo
Puigcerdá 8
28001 Madrid
Tel. 431 64 56
Excellent Basque-French cuisine. Closed Saturday lunchtime, Sunday, Holy Week and August.

El Bodegón
Pinar 15
28006 Madrid
Tel. 262 88 44
Closed Saturday lunchtime, Sunday, public holidays and August.

El Cenador del Prado
Prado 4
28014 Madrid
Tel. 429 15 49
Notably good cuisine. Pleasant restaurant. Closed Sunday and most of August.

Fortuny
Fortuny 34
28010 Madrid
Tel. 410 77 07
Small, elegantly decorated former palace. Pleasant terrace. Outdoor dining. Closed Saturday lunchtime, Sunday and public holidays.

Jockey
Amador de los Ríos 6
28010 Madrid
Tel. 419 24 35
Notably good cuisine. Elegant decor. Closed Sunday, public holidays and August.

La Fragata
Capitán Haya 45
28020 Madrid
Tel. 270 98 36
Dinner with music.

L'Albufera
Capitán Haya 45
28043 Madrid
Tel. 279 63 74; tlx. 23142
Meals accompanied by piano music. Closed August.

Las Cuatro Estaciones
General Ibañez Ibero 5
28003 Madrid
Tel. 253 63 05; tlx. 43709
Notably good cuisine. Modern decor. Closed Saturday, Sunday and August.

Lúculo
Génova 19
28005 Madrid
Tel. 419 40 29
Notably good cuisine. Closed Saturday lunchtime, Sunday, public holidays and mid-August to mid-September.

Lur Maitea
Fernando el Santo 4
28010 Madrid
Tel. 419 09 38
Basque cuisine. Closed Saturday lunchtime, public holidays and August.

Príncipe de Viana
Manuel de Falla 5
28036 Madrid
Tel. 259 14 48
Notably good Basque cuisine. Closed Saturday lunchtime, Sunday, Holy Week and August.

Senorío de Bertiz
Comandante Zorita 6
28020 Madrid
Tel. 233 27 57
Notably good cuisine. Closed Saturday lunchtime, Sunday, public holidays and August.

Zalacaín
Álvarez de Baena 4
28006 Madrid
Tel. 261 48 40
Superb cuisine. Elegant decor. Outdoor dining. Closed Saturday lunchtime, Sunday, Holy Week and August.

MEDIUM-PRICED
(ptas. 3,000–4,000)

A' Casinã
Puente de los Franceses
28040 Madrid
Tel. 449 05 76
Galician cuisine. Outdoor dining.

Ainhoa
Bárbara de Braganza 12
28004 Madrid
Tel. 410 54 55
Basque cuisine. Closed Sunday and August.

Amalur
Padre Damián 37
28036 Madrid
Tel. 457 62 97
*Closed Sunday, public holidays
and August.*

Bar del Teatro
Prim 5
28004 Madrid
Tel. 231 17 97
*Situated in a wine cellar. Closed
Saturday lunchtime and Sunday.*

Bogavente
Capitán Haya 20
28020 Madrid
Tel. 456 21 14
Fish and shellfish.

Combarro
Reina Mercedes 12
28020 Madrid
Tel. 254 77 84
*Galician cuisine. Closed Sunday
evening and August.*

Cota 13
estación de Chamartín
28036 Madrid
Tel. 315 52 18
*Outdoor dining. Closed Saturday,
Sunday, public holidays and
August.*

Currito
casa de Campo – Pabellón de
Vizcaya
28011 Madrid
Tel. 464 57 04
Basque cuisine. Outdoor dining.

El Espejo
paseo de Recoletos 31
28004 Madrid
Tel. 410 25 25
Replica of old Paris café.

El Fogón
Villanueva 34
28001 Madrid
Tel. 275 44 00; tlx. 22700
Rustic Spanish style.

El Landó
pl. Gabriel Miró 8
28005 Madrid
Tel. 266 76 81
*Elegant decor. Closed Sunday and
August.*

El Pescador
José Ortega y Gasset 75
28006 Madrid
Tel. 402 12 90
*Notably good cuisine. Fish and
shellfish. Closed Sunday and
mid-August to mid-September.*

Guipúzcoa
casa de Campo – Pabellón de
Guipúzcoa
28011 Madrid
Tel. 470 04 21
Basque cuisine. Outdoor dining.

Gure-Etxea
pl. de la Paja 12
28005 Madrid
Tel. 265 61 49
*Notably good, Basque cuisine.
Closed Sunday and August.*

Horcher
Alfonso XII – 6
28014 Madrid
Tel. 522 07 31
Notably good cuisine. Elegant decor.

Irizar
Jovellanos 3 – 1° piso
28014 Madrid
Tel. 231 45 69
Notably good, Basque-French cuisine. Closed Saturday lunchtime, Sunday and evenings of public holidays.

Jai-Alai
Balbina Valverde 2
28002 Madrid
Tel. 261 27 42
Basque cuisine. Outdoor dining. Closed Monday and mid-August to early September.

José Luis
Rafael Salgado 11
28036 Madrid
Tel. 250 02 42; tlx. 41779
Outdoor dining. Closed Sunday and August.

Korynto
Preciados 36
28013 Madrid
Tel. 521 59 65
Fish and shellfish.

Kulixka
Fuencarral 124
28010 Madrid
Tel. 447 25 38
Fish and shellfish.

La Boucade
Capitán Haya 30
28020 Madrid
Tel. 456 02 45
Closed Saturday lunchtime, Sunday, public holidays and August.

La Nueva Máquina
av. del Brasil 7
28020 Madrid
Tel. 455 10 02
Outdoor dining. Pleasant terrace. Closed Saturday lunchtime and Sunday.

Las Cuevas de Luis Candelas
Cuchilleros 1
28005 Madrid
Tel. 266 54 28
Old-Madrid decor. Waiters dressed as old-style bandits.

La Trainera
Lagasca 60
28001 Madrid
Tel. 276 80 35
Notably good cuisine. Fish and shellfish. Closed Sunday and August.

Los Borrachos de Velázquez
Principe de Vergara 205
28002 Madrid
Tel. 458 10 76
Andalusian restaurant. Closed Sunday.

Los Porches
paseo Pintor Rosales 1
28008 Madrid
Tel. 247 70 53
Outdoor dining.

Mayte Commodore
Serrano 145
28002 Madrid
Tel. 261 86 06
Elegant decor. Outdoor dining.
Closed Sunday.

Mesón El Caserío
Capitán Haya 49
28020 Madrid
Tel. 270 96 29
Rustic decor. Outdoor dining.

Moañā
Hileras 4
28013 Madrid
Tel. 248 29 14
Galician cuisine. Closed Sunday,
evenings of public holidays and
July.

Nuevo Valentín
av. Concha Espina 8
28036 Madrid
Tel. 259 74 16
Outdoor dining.

O'Pazo
Reina Mercedes 20
28020 Madrid
Tel. 234 37 48
Fish and shellfish. Closed Sunday
and August.

Ponteareas
Claudio Coello 96
28006 Madrid
Tel. 275 57 73
Galician cuisine.
Closed July, Sunday and public
holidays.

Posada de la Villa
Cava Baja 9
28005 Madrid
Tel. 266 18 80
Old inn in Castilian style. Closed
Sunday evening and August.

Rafa
Narváez 68
28009 Madrid
Tel. 273 10 87
Outdoor dining.

Sacha
Juan Hurtado de Mendoza 11
28036 Madrid
Tel. 457 51 52
Outdoor dining. Closed Sunday
and August.

St.-James
Juan Bravo 26
28020 Madrid
Tel. 275 60 10
Outdoor dining. Closed Sunday.

Schwarzwald (Selva Negra)
O'Donnell 46
28009 Madrid
Tel. 409 56 13
Original decor.

Taberna del Alabardero
Felipe V - 6
28013 Madrid
Tel. 247 25 77
Typical tavern.

Villa y Corte de Madrid
Serrano 110
28025 Madrid
Tel. 261 29 77
Elegant decor. Closed Sunday in
summer, and August.

Viridiana
Fundadores 23
28028 Madrid
Tel. 256 77 73
*Notably good cuisine. Closed
Sunday and August.*

LOWER-PRICED
(below ptas. 3,000)

Alejandro
Mesonero Romanos 7
28013 Madrid
Tel. 231 51 04
Outdoor dining. Closed Sunday.

Alkalde
Jorge Juan 10
28001 Madrid
Tel. 276 33 59
*Situated in a wine cellar. Closed
Saturday evening and Sunday in
July, and August.*

Antonio
Santa Engracia 54
28010 Madrid
Tel. 447 40 68
*Closed Sunday night, Monday
and August.*

Asador Guetaria
Comandanta Zorita 8
28020 Madrid
Tel. 254 66 32
*Rustic Basque-style decor. Basque
cuisine. Closed Sunday and
August.*

Aymar
Fuencarral 138
28010 Madrid
Tel. 445 57 67
Fish and shellfish.

Bodegón Navarro
paseo de la Castellana 121
28046 Madrid
Tel. 455 30 11
Rustic decor. Closed Sunday.

Botín
Cuchilleros 17
28005 Madrid
Tel. 266 42 17
*Typical wine cellar in old-Madrid
style.*

Café de Oriente (Horno de Leña)
pl. Oriente 2
28013 Madrid
Tel. 247 15 64
Situated in a wine cellar.

Casa Domingo
Alcalá 99
28009 Madrid
Tel. 431 18 95
Outdoor dining.

Casa Lucio
Cava Baja 35
28005 Madrid
Tel. 265 32 52
*Castilian decor. Closed Saturday
lunchtime and August.*

Café Viena
Luisa Fernanda 23
28008 Madrid
Tel. 248 15 91
*Meals accompanied by piano
music. Replica of an old-style
café. Closed Saturday lunchtime,
Sunday and August.*

Casa Félix
Bréton de los Herreros 39
28003 Madrid
Tel. 441 24 79

Casa gallega
pl. de San Miguel 8
28005 Madrid
Tel. 247 30 55
Galician cuisine.

El Asador de Aranda
pl. de Castilla 3
28046 Madrid
Tel. 733 87 02
Roast lamb a speciality. Castilian decor. Closed Sunday evening and August.

El Hostal
Principe de Vergara 285
28016 Madrid
Tel. 259 11 94
Closed Sunday.

Hogar Gallego
pl. Comandante Las Morenas 3
28013 Madrid
Tel. 248 64 04
Outdoor dining. Galician cuisine. Closed Sunday evening.

La Fonda
Lagasca 11
28001 Madrid
Tel. 403 83 07
Catalan cuisine.

La Plaza de Chamberí
pl. de Chamberí 10
28010 Madrid
Tel. 446 06 97
Outdoor dining. Closed Sunday and Holy Week.

Las Cumbres
Alberto Alcocer 32
28036 Madrid
Tel. 458 76 92
Andalusian tavern.

Las Cumbres
av. de América 33
28002 Madrid
Tel. 413 07 51
Andalusian tavern. Closed Sunday evening.

Las Reses
Orfila 3
28010 Madrid
Tel. 419 10 13
Meat specialities. Closed Sunday, public holidays and August.

Los Galayos
Botoneras 5
28012 Madrid
Tel. 266 30 28
Outdoor dining.

Lucca
José Ortega y Gasset 29
28006 Madrid
Tel. 276 01 44
Modern decor. Meals accompanied by piano music.

Mesón Auto
paseo de la Chopera 71
28045 Madrid
Tel. 239 66 00
Rustic decor.

México Lindo
pl. República del Ecuador 4
28016 Madrid
Tel. 259 48 33
Mexican cuisine.

O'Xeito
paseo de la Castellana 47
28046 Madrid
Tel. 419 83 87
Galician-style decor. Fish and shellfish. Closed Saturday lunchtime, Sunday and August.

Pizzería Paolo
General Rodrigo 3
28003 Madrid
Tel. 254 44 28
Italian cuisine. Closed Sunday and August.

Salvador
Barbieri 12
28004 Madrid
Tel. 521 45 24
With paintings and photos of the bullfighting world. Closed Sunday and mid-July to early September.

Sixto
José Ortega y Gasset 83
28006 Madrid
Tel. 402 15 83
Outdoor dining. Closed Sunday evening.

Sixto Gran Mesón
Cervantes 28
28014 Madrid
Tel. 429 22 55
Castilian decor. Closed Sunday evening.

Taberna Carmencita
Libertad 16
28004 Madrid
Tel. 231 66 12
Typical tavern. Closed Sunday.

Toralla
Amador de los Ríos 8
28010 Madrid
Tel. 410 28 88
Galician cuisine. Closed Saturday evening and Sunday.